THE
GULLAH

"People Blessed by God"

Llaila Olela Afrika

Published by *A&B PUBLISHERS GROUP* · 1000 Atlantic Avenue · Brooklyn, N.Y. 11238

ISBN: 1-886433-01-1
formerly
ISBN: 1-877610-02-X

COVER DESIGN: *Llaila O. Afrika*
ILLUSTRATION: *Logan Kline.*

10 09 08 07   6 5 4 3 2
Printed in the United States

THE
GULLAH

A&B Publishers Group
Brooklyn,
New York, 11238

Dedicated to:

My wife, Aseelah
My Son, Maideah and
My Daughter, Naima

To schedule lectures, obtain copies of videos on over
fifty topics or for copies of this and other books.
Write to

Llaila Afrika
P.O Box 2475
Beaufort, SC 29901

CONTENTS

ABOUT THE AUTHOR

Llaila Olela Afrika is a Naturopathist, Historian, Certified Addictionologist, Auricular Acupuncturist, Medical Astrologist, author, and lecturer. Naturopathy is the science of treating diseases with herbs, vitamins and minerals, and other natural remedies. His naturopathic background includes a unique blend of nutritional history and of African history.

Llaila provides lively invigorating lectures on more than 60 different health topics and other topics, such as African American history, relationship, Gullah history and culture, Gullah folk remedies, and Ancient Africa. His lectures are informative and inspirational. They always include a slide film and/or overhead projector presentation.

OTHER BOOKS BY THE AUTHOR

African Holistic Health
A complete herb remedy guide, disease treatments, nutrition, foods that kill, self-diagnosis, charts, sex laws, herpes and AIDS treatments, cocaine detox, African herb history.

Nutricide—The Nutritional Destruction of the Black Race
Reveals the harmful effects of foods, computers, commercials, food addiction, etc. It has the correct growth and development schedule for Black children, the nutritional cause of homosexuality, hyperactivity, racism, etc.

ABOUT THE GULLAH FESTIVAL

The Gullah Festival of South Carolina, Inc., a nonprofit, tax-exempt organization of Beaufort, South Carolina, was established for the purpose of having an annual three-day celebration of the historically significant Sea Island heritage. Its goal is to reclaim for future generations the beauty and mystery of the disappearing Gullah culture—compelling mix of West African legacy and American experience.

The festival showcases gospel, jazz, a Bible translation into the Gullah language, traditional games, stories originated in Africa, fine arts display, folklore, and arts and crafts. The Gullah Festival has constructed a firm foundation in the understanding of Gullah heritage and culture, and has creatively responded to a very visible need. The festival is held annually on the weekend preceding Memorial Day.

This book, *The Gullah*, contains a compilation of little-known facts by our historian, Llaila O. Afrika.

For further information about the festival, write:

Ms. Rosalie F. Pazant
President and Co-founder
The Gullah Festival of South Carolina, Inc.
P.O. Box 83
Beaufort, SC   29901

For handbags, T-Shirts, and other items with the official Gullah logo, contact the above address.

INTRODUCTION

The Sea Islands are a chain of islands in the Atlantic Ocean off the East Coast of North America. These islands extend from northern Florida to the coasts of Georgia, South Carolina and North Carolina.

The Sea Islands are unique because they are the home of African prisoners of the Race War (slaves) from West Africa, the Congo area and the African interior, called "Gullah."

The origin of the word, "Gullah," is mixed and varied. "Gull" may mean God, and "ah" is a word placed before or after a word. It usually refers to a blessing. This would mean that "Gullah" could be translated as "the blessing of God," or "the people blessed by God." Many African communal names refer to God or praise God. Further, the Gullah have been related to the Gola and a mixture of central, southern and Africans that had skills (technology needed for slavery were shipped from ports of Sierra Leone and other ports. The Vai people, or Gala, or Gallinas (another word for Vai) are believed to be the African connection for the Gullah people in this hemisphere. With these African connections, the Sea Islands Gullah have always demonstrated the meaning of Gullah by being steadfast in their Africanity, and by always standing with God.

Gullah is a title created by whites and given to Africans that lived near the sea and/or rivers. The Gullah area includes Tidewater, Virginia, parts of the Chesapeake Bay, and extends 50 miles inland, continuing down the east coast to Mayport, Florida. The titles Gullah, Trinidadian, Jamaican, Puerto Rican, Latino, Creole, etc., were created by whites to keep Africans mistrustful and divided from each other. Within this deafricanization is the White Supremacy belief that light-skinned Africans and Africans with Caucasoid physical features or lifestyles are better off (superior) and beautiful. Historically, Gullah people were captured from many areas of Africa and especially the Rice Coast of West Africa. The technologically advanced Africans had many counterattacks (so-called rebellions) on the continent of Africa, on ships and plantations. They were forcefully brought to the Sea Islands because the Europeans were without resources, land, labor, and the technology needed to build their wealth, empires and American colonies.

The Gullah captives possessed skills (technology) in agriculture, science, military science, tool making, bookkeeping, cabinet making, furniture making, construction, banking, government, teaching, and most of all, they had over 10,000 years of culture in the most developed civilization in the world—that of Africa. It is the African technology that produced European and European-American wealth. The Europeans maintain their wealth by owning and controlling the United States of America through the Federal Reserve. The Internal Revenue Service illegally collects taxes and gives the money to a privately-owned business called the Federal Reserve. This foreign company gained its power from slavery and control the price of money in order to control the American economy and military, and thereby, European control of America and Africa. This could not have been done without the money gained from slavery (European type of welfare).

During colonial times, the European-Americans tried unsuccessfully to profit from southern natural resources. However, without African technology, they

During colonial times, the European-Americans tried unsuccessfully to profit from southern natural resources. However, without African technology, they failed. American Indians were enslaved by Europeans. This slavery was unproductive because the Native Americans had labor but little technology for the type of work required. The colonials then tried to enslave white indentures. This also gave them labor but no technology that they could use to build wealth. Finally, the Europeans attempted slavery with the Africans. This gave them labor and technology. Thus, African chattel slavery, when engaged, was an economic success for the European. The knowledge needed for farming and building in the Sea Islands required specialized skills that were found in abundance in West Africa. The rape of Africa for people with these skills inadvertently created a geographical area in the Sea Islands, uniquely African, and inhabited by a strong and proud African people. The Melanin dominate African race has the most blood circulation to all types of skin (derma); absorbs more flavor from food; sees and hears full spectrum color and sound/music; body contains the highest quantity of vitamins and minerals; vibrates more electromagnetic energy; has the fastest nerve and muscle response; possesses the highest brain activity; and is the most psychic, spiritual and civilized people —"the people blessed by God."

The Gullah captives produced high profits for the Europeans. These slaves were not brought from the mainland or mixing ports. They were brought directly from Africa to the islands. To get the maximum labor output from these Africans, the Europeans isolated them. The Gullah were prized possessions as "slaves" and sold at higher prices than other Africans, which further justified their isolation. During this period of enslavement, the Gullah were left on the Sea Islands to themselves except for overseers (white supervisors). The planters (plantation owners) lived on the mainland and made periodic visits to the islands to check on crop production and on the "seasonin" and breeding of the Gullah slave livestock (stocks) and bondage (bonds).

The isolation of the Gullah from mainland whites and other Africans allowed the Gullah to maintain a high degree of African culture. African culture is not merely an ethnic group of people that have the same rituals, ceremonies, history and experience in common. African culture and history primarily serves to help its people solve problems (i.e., economic, social, spiritual, and military) adapt and to improve their society and self. The high concentration of Africans on the islands allowed a Gullah Community to form (an Afrocentric cultural entity within a European-American cultural context). Further, after the end of the European inter-tribal war (Civil War), the Gullah remained isolated from whites from 1861 to 1930. During 1930, a bridge was built that connected the mainland to the islands. Since that time, whites have continued to infiltrate these historical, ancestral and African American owned lands.

For many years, the Gullah have been noted for their speech patterns and English language usage. The Gullah "accent" is much more than a West African accent on English. Oddly enough, English is basically a mixture of German words and bastardized Latinized African words. It is not actually a language, but more of a degenerated European form of Euronics (i.e., Ebonics). Gullah is an African language that uses African word order and conceptual meanings. In other words, the Gullah language is uniquely African, with English words added to it. In addition to the Gullah language, the Gullah people have a lifestyle and a her-itage that has left its mark on American and world history.

The following pages contain little-known facts about the Gullah contribution to human history. These facts are not only a listing of events and dates; but also an intriguing glimpse into human struggle, and into the growth and development of a people through enslave-ment and beyond slavery.

Where Gullahs Come From

The majority of the African Americans (all Gullahs) came from the urban cities of West Africa. The urban cities' area covered 2.5 million square miles, which is the size of the United States. West Africa is an area of low country grassland (three-fourths of it) and not a desert or jungle area. The area is similar to the Sea Island and East coastal states of Southern America. The 200 to 300 cities of urban Africa had walls built around them. Within the major walls would be other circular walls with distances of up to three-quarter miles apart. Some of the large cities would cover an area the size of Texas with a single castle covering 640 acres.

The walls were up to 100 miles in circular length, 40 to 50 feet in height and 30 feet wide and had farms, lakes, storage buildings and stables of over 1,000 horses, donkeys or camels. An African walled city would be divided into over 120 wards or districts with each district having a mayor. Small towns and surrounding suburban areas or villages were part of the large city. The cities had paved streets up to 300 feet wide, two-story buildings with glass windows, stores, colleges, churches and no police and no jails.

African cities were built to reflect the laws of God, nature and man. The family was the foundation of African cities and served to holistically (spirit, mind, body) influence an individual's behavior and thus control the cities.

The large urban metropolitan cities were part of many African countries such as Sierra Leone, Benin, Ghana, Liberia and Ivory Coast. Many smaller cities such as Jenne, Kumasi, Segu, and Ife plus towns and villages were part of great empires such as Mali, Bornu, Kong, Mossi and Asante empires. These cities date back as far as 1 A.D. Mandara, 9 A.D. Kanem-Bornu, 1100 Katsina, 1350 Gobir and up to the 18th century. They had many industries in shipbuilding, metal, textile, commerce, literature, medicine and imported and exported to Asia and the Americas. Some cities had populations of 400,000 people with over 70,000 men a day commuting to work in craft and technical factories or to agricultural fields of millet, wheat, corn, plantain, rice and cotton.

The cities were invaded by the Europeans in the 13th century. Historically, the ancient Greeks never claimed to be a part of Europe nor were they a part of ancient Europe. Ancient Greeks said the Europeans were barbarians, savages, infidels, and cave dwellers. When the Europeans captured Greece, they claimed Greek culture as the root of their own culture. Europe came into existence after the fall of the Mediterranean countries of Greece and Rome. Europeans used biological warfare (diseases), chemicals (drugs and alcohol), spiritual (forced to adopt European religions), psychological (made to feel inferior), and military warfare (guns, rockets, bombs) to defeat Africa. It is estimated that 500,000,000 Africans and African Americans (includes Gullahs) were killed by the invasions, colonialism and slavery business. For more on urban Africa, read *African Cities and Towns Before the European Conquest*, by Richard Hull and *Urban Heritage of West Africa*, by Daud M. Watts.

GULLAH
LANGUAGE PATH

The Gullah language distribution path was in many areas largely due to the need for the technology of these West African slaves. These African prisoners of war were (African countries fought for 400 years to stop the European invasion) sold from Louisiana to Charleston.

The cargo ships loaded with slaves and cargo would start in European countries, such as Ireland, England, France, Spain, Italy, and Portugal. Then they would go to Africa, the Canary Islands, Cape Verde, across the Atlantic Ocean to South America, Haiti, Barbados, Hispaniola, and Cuba. They would also go on to the Gulf of Mexico, which includes Louisiana and Alabama. From there, they went on to the Bahamas, the Gullah slave-concentrated areas of the Sea Islands (Florida, Georgia, South and North Carolina), and then Bermuda.

Today, there is still a common linguistic connection with West Africans in the above parts of the world.

The Gullah

Above: Many slaves spent the entire voyage from Africa to
America in positions similar to this.

Slave Barracks

Gullah
Medu Netcher

The ancient Africans originally came to the Americas around 5000 BC and brought with them plants, technology, culture, and language. The early American Quachita natives were probably from the Mali region of Africa and related to the Mende. They taught the Native Americans technology, military science, music, words, culture, religion, and influenced the clothing styles of the ancient Natives. Many of their contributions are erroneously attributed to the Native Americans. For example, the African Moors (Ethiopians) introduced music to Spain. Consequently, African harmonies and rhythms are erroneously called Latin music. The Quachitas lived on 3 million acres of land that covered part of areas in Texas, Mississippi, Louisiana, Arkansas, and Oklahoma. The Jamassi (Yamesee) African peoples lived in the Carolinas, Sea Islands, Florida, and Georgia. The so-called Carib ancient Africans lived in Mexico, the Caribbean, and South and Central Americas. These ancient Africans traded goods with Africans on the continent long before Europeans discovered America. It is erroneously assumed that their style of clothing, words, and music is Native

American. The Europeans called these Africans very dark skinned Indians and named them Black Foot, Tar Heels, Brass Ankles, etc. These ancient Africans constructed Pyramids, High-rise apartment buildings and cities with African technology.

Ancient Africans, born in America and those that came to America before Columbus, introduced African words. For example the African Medu Netcher words Neb = Lord, Ra = God, which combines to form the word Metro (Ruling Place); Ma'i (Maat) = Justice; Ur (or) = order which combines to form the English word Mayor = Keeper of Order; Sala = garden which mistranslates to the English word salad; the nine Fauts (Gods) who decide upon who is to blame for wrong behavior, which translates to the English word, Fault; A-Meru (Amir) = Leader, Kas = Life, combines to form America (Leader of Life).

The primitive Europeans, such as the Greeks and Romans arrived in Africa with a limited vocabulary of very few words. Their few "grunt" sounding words reflected their Ice Age development. They were "Hun" = without spirit or food and called themselves Hungry, Hungarians, Hunters, etc. They had trouble pronouncing the cluster vowels and the "L" and "R" of African language. This lead to mispronunciations and mistranslations. In other words, the Europeans speak a primitive Euronics (i.e., Ebonics). The so-called Africanism in the Gullah language is incorrect. There is Africanism in European language. Primitive Europeans stole African words, mispronounced them, Latinized them, and called them Latin words. English, as well as American English, is a dialect consisting of combinations of German words mixed with Latinized Medu Netcher. English is not by definition a language, but a form of bastardized African words. Europeans have a criminal relationship with Africans and have stolen African words, culture, resources, music, technology and African people (slaves). In their attempt to use their Left Mind, (Rational, Logical, Intellectual part of the brain) they have failed to construct a true language.

Their Left-Minded ability is inadequate and undeveloped. For example, they constructed a school system that fails them, agriculture that chemically pollutes the environment and causes diseases, an economic system that creates poverty, a legal system that punishes the innocent and a so-called language that has over 400 negative connotations for the word Black (Black Monday, Black Mail, Black Humor, Black Lie, Blacken Your Name, Black Cat, Black Ball, Black List, etc.)

Medu Netcher words are the foundation words of the African peoples languages. The attempt to deny the Medu Netcher and the Congolese (Sudan area) words in Gullah and to associate it with just the coast of Africa tend to deny the African origin of words and civilization.

SEA ISLAND INDIANS

The territory called Carolinas was called Chicora by the Native Americans, just as Africa was called Ake Bu Lan by its natives. The Indians were misused, mistreated, abused, exploited, and denied use of their own land. Many of them moved away from the European invaders. However, some Indians lived near the Europeans and were culturally disenfranchised. Those groups were racially mixed (African Indians, Afro-American Indians, and Euro-Indians). Groups such as the Catawba lived on the pitiful wilderness ghetto, called a reservation, in York County, South Carolina. In the 1930 census, Croatians (also called Turks, Brass Ankles and Redbones) were identified. The early African voyages and contact (came to America before Columbus) is evident in cultures of the Creeks, Cherokee, Chickasaw, and Choctaw. The Indian inhabitants of the islands such as the Gaule, Cusabo, and then the Yemasses were killed, domesticated or sold as slaves. Yemasses (Yamesse) along with other Black Native Americans were described as having thick lips, woolly hair, and black skin by early European explorers (invaders. Early Europeans only knew of one

9

group of Black people those that lived in India (Untouchables). Therefore, they called the Africans—Indians. The Sea Islands Indians were courageous and became a part of Gullah Island history and are so noted in this book. It is interesting to note that some of the Europeans that the Indians, as well as the Gullahs met, were not noble people. The State of Georgia was founded as a European prisoner colony = prison state. European countries used America (and the Sea Islands) as dumpsites for social waste. Cargoes of social waste such as criminals, orphans, whores, the homeless, welfare recipients, the diseased, and the mentally ill were loaded on ships called "The Ship of Fools" and sent to America. Additionally, European-Americans sought refuge on the islands, such as Aaron Burr on St. Simeon's Island after killing Alexander Hamilton. Oddly enough, Edgar Allen Poe was inspired to write" The Golden Bug" while on Sullivans Island, near Charleston. The Indians were forcefully subjected to the worst of European society and yet have survived and have fought with the Gullahs against the European's oppression. The Indians are truly a great nation of colored people.

Today, the United States government refuses to recognize the Edisto Indians as Native Americans and will not register them with the Bureau of Indian Affairs and will not allow them to practice many parts of their culture.

The cargo ships loaded with slaves and cargo would start in European countries, such as Ireland, England, France, Spain, Italy, and Portugal. Then they would go to Africa, the Canary Islands, Cape Verde, across the Atlantic Ocean to South America, Haiti, Barbados, Hispaniola and Cuba. They would also go on to the Gulf of Mexico, which includes Louisiana and Alabama. From there, they went on to the Bahamas, the Gullah slave-concentrated areas of the Sea Islands (Florida, Georgia, South and North Carolina) and then Bermuda. There is still a common linguistic connection with West Africans in parts of the world that were part of the slave trade-shipping route.

Gullah warrior from runaway slave
communities attacked whites

Original indigeneous Chief John Horse
led attacks on U.S. troops, Black Seminole
Indians (Africans), and Gullah Runaways

Amazing Facts About the Gullah People and the Sea Islands

1. **1461**—Sir Henry, the Navigator of France usurped the African ship building techniques, designs and sailing methods. He used the sale of slaves to finance construction of the new designed ships that could come close to shore, move fast, and carry large slave cargoes (300-400). These ships ignited the slave trade, which eventually brought the Gullahs to America.

2. **1477**—Christopher Columbus (a Jew raised in Italy, hired by Spain) came to the Sea Islands before he reached any other land in this hemisphere. He was a Portuguese Jew involved in the slave trade before he came to America. He started working in the slave trade at age 14. Columbus was responsible for the murdering of thousands of Africans and Native Americans. He did not discover America. In recorded history, in 1296, Mansu Musa III, of Africa, was sending ships back and forth to the Americas before the American Indians and Columbus arrived.

3. **1500**—The concept of "Wonderland" brought to America by the Gullahs. An African concept "Gondwanland" (English, wonderland) is the idea of paradise on Earth. It is also the name given to a single land mass (World Island) that all continents were a part of before they drifted apart, which created Africa, the Americas, etc. The rites of passage fairy tale, "Alice in Wonderland" alludes to Gondwanland.

4. **1500**—The oldest people in America, the Gullahs were estimated to live to be 140 to 200 years of age.

5. **1500**—The beginning of the deliberate destruction of the African Babysitting Art (Kindezi), similar to preschools and included teaching. The Babysitters (Ndezi) included the youth and elderly. They freely babysitted between different families and tribes and helped to maintain cultural harmony amongst Gullahs and other Africans.

6. **1500**—The European ganus (gangs) tribal ethnic social groups evolved to the tribal feudal caste system. The landless gangs' labor was exploited by the ruling landlords. This created the first welfare system for the rich. The African chattel slaves were put in work gangs for the house, fields and skilled crafts. This was similar to European gangs with one exception, Africans were denied the right to use their culture, language, religion, and clothes. They were also classified as animals, bred, and branded with the approval of European religions.

7. **1500**—The use of the custom of leaving glasses, mirrors, dishes, and shining objects on graves is an African custom used to help

the deceased travel to the heavens. Gullahs continued the custom of leaving a meal (dinner) on the grave or the porch for the deceased.

8. 1500—First to use the "Chain of Death" or the "Chains of Bad Luck" ritual. Gullahs would break glasses, mirrors, bottles, or dishes in order to stop a chain of bad luck or death. Europeans, typically break a martini glass in a fireplace to break the chain of bad luck.

9. 1500—Many of the African military scientists (warriors) that fought counterattacks (rebellions, revolts, etc.) against the Europeans were called "The People Who Could Fly." This referred to African Martial Artist Capoeira (Judo, Kung Fu), who seem to fly high in the air in order to do kicks. The Europeans had never seen Martial Arts nor could they do it. The first Martial Artists were African.

Ancient Egyptian mural from Beni Hasan
(Martial Arts)

10. 1510—First contemporary West Africans in America came to the Sea Islands. They trav-

15

eled to St. Augustine, Florida with Ponce De Leon. These were free Africans who never experienced slavery.

11.   1520—First American islands to be renamed after a saint. Gordillo landed at Coffin's Point on Good Friday and named the grouping of islands, St. Helena. It included the areas from Edisto, South Carolina to Savannah, Georgia.

12.   1520—First Native Americans kidnaped. Gordillo kidnaped Yemassees, and attempted to take them to Europe. His ship sank and all the Yemassees he had stolen, drowned.

13.   1520—Lucas Vasquez de Ayllon came to the Sea Islands in search of Gullahs who were skilled in mining and agriculture. He took them to Santo Domingo, South America.

14.   1523—First outbreak of a major contagious disease. More than 500 Africans died of diseases they caught from Europeans. This epidemic happened at Cape Fear, North Carolina.

15.   1526—First pigs brought to America arrived at Parris Island with De Ayllon.

16.   1526—First contemporary African Americans born were on St. Catherine's Island. First Gullah rebellion that led to their liberation and freedom occurred on St. Catherine's Island.

17.   1526—First major U.S. city abandoned was Winyah Bay City on St. Helena Island.

18. 1562—Captain John Hawkins (1532-1595) captured 300 Africans from Sierra Leone. Some were able to return to their homeland.

19. 1563—First ship built in America, by Europeans, was patterned after an African ship design. The Yemassees helped Nicholas Barro's men design and build it.

20. 1563—Cannibalism on St. Helena Island. Jean Ribaut, a Frenchman, and his crew ran out of food and began eating human flesh. The African Egyptians of the 9th Dynasty also recorded white cannibalism in Europe in 3000 B.C.

21. 1565—The use of "Pit and Pebble" games in America. The European games of baseball, marbles, football, tennis, pocket pool, basketball, and golf are all forms of the ancient African Pit and Pebble games that the Gullah and ancient Africans played.

22. 1566—Fort San Felipe was built on Parris Island by the Spanish.

23. 1566—Whites forcefully taught the Catholic religion to Native Americans occurred on Parris Island. Gullah slaves were herded and whipped to church like cattle until they submitted to the European idea of God.

24. 1587—Spain purchased the first Native American captives ("slaves"). Later, in history, Native Americans would have African slaves.

25. 1600—First Christmas holidays. Gullah captives were allowed to sell goods, seafood and their labor to others and keep the earnings. The slave master introduced drinking alcohol as a way to celebrate on Fridays and Christmas. The

Gullahs performed the "Jehuti" ritual whereby the Elder slaves used a mock Septer (cane), Eye of Heru Hat (Raccoon Hat) and Ankh (Christian Cross) and would lead the slaves in a ritual march to the Big House to collect coins in a cup from each white. The coins symbolized the value of the whites' souls on judgement day.

26.   1600— "Silly" stories told by the Gullahs. "Jelle" tales were told by the Sierra Leone Gullahs. These were tall tales that required much acting out and pantomime, and were called "acting silly" (Jelle) by whites.

27.   1600—Galee or African head wrap used by Gullah women. Later they straightened their hair by using heated forks. Men used axle grease or cut their hair very short so that their hair would not show curliness (kinky) and shaved a part in the hair so that it could resemble the white male's hair (straight and limp).

28.   1600—First "cowboys." Gullah captives from Ghana and from the Gambia River (Senegal), were brought to the Sea Islands because they were expert horsemen and herdsmen.

29.   1600—Use of Brer Rabbit stories. These were trickster tales based on an intelligent hero that outwitted the forces of the unknown or supernatural; typical of African Ashanti spider tales.

30.   1600—Bricklayers and Masons technology of Gullahs was used in construction. Spain learned of this skill from West Africans during the time Mansa Musa made his famous pilgrimage to Mecca (1324-1325). Spain would later pay high prices for skilled Gullah captives.

African Tabby construction skills of Gullahs
(SCPRT)

31.   1600—Slaves were given seven years to live! Portuguese enslavers predicted that Gullah captives would live seven years and then drop dead from physical exhaustion. It was also feared that if slavery did not end or if the slaves did not die from exhaustion, then they would be a majority in America.

32.   1600—The Sea Islands were the first areas to maintain the African Secret Societies of Poro, for men, and Sande, for women. These were called "Bush" schools. They learned the "Rites of Passage" and also how to revolt.

33.   1600—Africans were branded with hot irons that cooked the flesh. These brands were called "Country Scars" or "Country Mark"and helped to keep track of freedom-seeking Africans.

34.   1600—Gullahs were first to use the "Chevron" to rank position. The military now uses it for noncommissioned officer ranking. Secret societies of Poro and Sande used chevron-type markings during initiation rituals to show step-by-step progressions.

These marks were cut on the skin of the cheek of the face.

35.   1600—Gullahs were first purchased for technological skills as metal workers, agricultural experts, barrel makers, bricklayers, swamp fishermen, cotton quilt weavers (quilted without stitching), and for other needed skills, such as herdsmen, deep sea divers, herbalists, and chemists.

36.   1600 (circa)—First nondenominational church established by the Gullahs called the Praise House. Praise Houses are found on every plantation in the Sea Islands. They sing and dance in a circle with a meditation trance called "Ring Shout." African dances copied by Europeans are Quizomba (Samba), Tangana (Tango), Charleston, Boogie Woogie, Rhumba, etc. Jazz dancing is dance performed to the African music, called Jazz. Jazz is a negative term. Europeans originally called it "Jackass Music," which eventually became the word, Jazz. A similar type word is picnic, which originally meant "pick a Nigger" and lynch him. Whites would bring families, food, and children, put table clothes on the ground, eat, and drink alcohol while watching a lynching.

37.   1600 (circa)—Many exceptionally physically built or intelligent or skilled Gullahs and other slaves were sold to slave breeding farms in Virginia, Maryland and Kentucky. Today, these states have switched to breeding horses for horse races. Some slaves were too crippled, damaged, diseased, or too old to do harsh work. They were sold at reduced rates at Refuse (Trash) Sales or Scramble Sales (Blue Light). Mr. J. Marion Sims, M.D. (Father of gynecology), bought such female slaves to practice operations (i.e., hysterec-

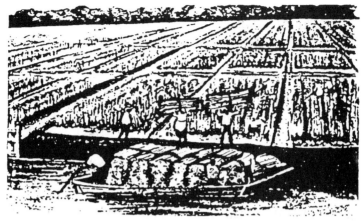

African rice cultivation skills of Gullahs
(SCPRT)

tomies). Many African ladies died. Children were often used to herd and whip work gangs of Refuse Slaves.

38.   **1600**—First African chants used in America (later called Gospel) were used by Gullahs. These were used at weddings, on holidays, at funerals, births, and at many other ceremonies.

39.   **1600**—Experts in irrigation systems. Gullah workers had skills in complex irrigation systems using dams, ditches, and sluices. These Africans were purchased directly from Africa's "Rice Coast" or the "Windward Coast" (the areas of Senegal, Sierra Leone, and Liberia).

40.   **1600** (circa)—First African American community to use "The Silent Trade" based on the honesty of the buyer and seller. Goods were sold without seeing the customer. For example, an owner would leave his store and leave items for sale. The customer could come at any time, pick up the goods and leave payment. The goods and money were never stolen. "The Silent Trade" was used in Mali, Songhay, Ghana, Sudan, Ethiopia, etc.

41. **1600** (circa)—"Basket Names" were given, by Elders, to infants and children that identified their Ancestral Spirit, Mission in Life, etc. A "Nickname" is given later in a person's life by a friend or relative and usually are based on personality characteristics.

42. **1600**—Palm leaf brooms were made by Gullahs. These were of African origin as is the art of Sea Islands basket weaving. The brooms are used to keep away evil spirits. Palm leaves were walked upon during fertility rituals.

43. **1600**—The word "Nigger" was used in reference to Gullahs from the Niger Bend or the Niger River area of Africa.

44. **1600**—Largest tabby fort in America, Fort Frederick, was located off the shore of the Broad River on a peninsula between Beaufort and Port Royal.

45. **1626**—African Gullah captives (slaves) were brought to Algoinga Island (Native American name for Sea Islands) off the coast of Turtle Island (Native American name for America).

46. **1640**—Use of African navigation and astrological principles used by the Gullahs. The "Drinking Gourd," called the "Big Dipper" by whites was referred to when crossing the Atlantic Ocean.

47. **1670**—One of the first cities in America was established at Port Royal. The site for this

city was later moved because of Spanish attacks. It is now called Charleston, South Carolina.

48. 1670—First English colonial settlement in South Carolina relocated in Charleston.

49. 1670—Planters using Gambian herdsmen (cowboys) said to raise cattle on the Sea Islands is as cheap as raising chickens.

50. 1670—First contemporary female doctors, in America, were Gullah women, so-called herbalists. They were Priestesses, Warriors and Midwives and often organized slave rebellions.

51. 1670—Indians were exported as slaves and half-breeds (mixed with West Africans). These Indians that were half Gullah were believed to yield a better species.

52. 1670—Disease used as a weapon to destroy Indians. The death rate of Indians (Coosaw, Creek, Yemassee, Cherokee) increased due to contact with diseased Sea Island Europeans.

53. 1671—Indian slaves bought with Gullah slave labor. The price for Indian slaves was paid with rice, turpentine, deer skins, pine, and pigs.

54. 1672—New Yorkers moved to Sea Islands to get in on financial profits of Gullah slavery. Dutch settlers from New York came to the Carolinas.

55. 1680—Madagascar Africans taught Dr. Henry of Beaufort agricultural knowledge.

He subsequently utilized West Africans to start rice farming in Beaufort County.

56. 1683—Gullah slave rustling was very profitable. Sea rustlers (pirates) increased stealing slaves in Carolina and made such profits from stealing West African slaves that they were able to retire in Carolina.

57. 1700—The newspaper, *Carolina Gazette*, reported that the General Assembly bought an African-trained Gullah doctor (herbalist), named Caesar because he cured diseases. Later, it became illegal for Euro-American doctors and drug stores to use African-trained Gullah doctors in their practices.

58. 1700—First on-the-job injuries were recorded. Planters allowed work-related injuries to go untreated. Female workers suffered from "Craw-Craw," which was a pustules itch. "Craw-Yaws" was a painful infection of the palms and soles.

59. 1700—Usage of African recipes: "Joll of rice,"a red rice, okra, fish gumbo; "Agidi," a boiled corn pasta, and "Fufu," a wheat porridge.

60. 1700—The Gullahs had the first African American private schools, called "Bush Schools" or "Sacred Grove Schools."

61. 1700—Gullahs would paint their doors royal blue as found in the Pyramid of Giza. This symbolized the highest order of wisdom and the worship of God.

62. 1700—Positive-thinking usage. "The Root Doctor" or "Doctor Buzzard" used the power of positive thinking concept in order to help

a person to believe in the things that they desired, i.e., escaping slavery, avoiding bad luck, illness or getting money. It was believed that the doctor could stop buzzards from waiting for you to die. In modern times, this concept was popularized by Norman Vincent Peale.

63. 1700—More than 200 Black soldiers from Haiti were sent by Toussaint L'Ouverture to help liberate Gullahs. These soldiers relocated in Nova Scotia.

64. 1700—Captain Paul Coffee started a Back-to-Africa movement and shipped former slaves and slaves home.

65. 1701—Profits from Gullah enslavement were used by the East India Company to found Yale University in Connecticut.

66. 1702—Sea Island Native American community stolen. The English, during Queen Anne's war, wanted more Native American workers (slaves), so they stole an entire Creek community.

67. 1702—The French paid some Cherokees to murder Conchak Emika, a Choctaw. English, French and Spanish tried to get Indians to fight on their sides by instigating wars between various Indian tribes and using espionage tactics (murdering and scalping Indians).

68. 1712— "No knock" search and seizure law. Gullah homes were searched every 14 days during captivity (slavery).

69. 1714—Tea came to the Sea Islands' colonists. However, a favored drink was a popular Gullah

mixture made from the cocoa bean (hot chocolate).

70.   1714—High taxes charged for pure Africans in South Carolina due to the technology (skills) they possessed.

71.   1715—The Yemassee War was fought. This was the first war in which combined Native American nations fought against the whites. The Creeks, Choctaws, Catawbas and Yemassees joined forces and battled the whites in the largest and most costly war in Carolina history. They continued their self-defense war from Edisto to St. Augustine until 1728.

72.   1717—Colonials first protest against England. Five-hundred seventy-three Negro slaves bought at 40 pounds (English money) tax per slave, caused the protest. Tax was high because slaves were skilled (Gullah).

73.   1718—"Slave" rustling pirate was captured in the Sea Islands. Captain Teach or "Blackbeard" was the famous rustler.

74.   1732—North Carolina was mostly established by Virginia tabacco businessmen and it also served as a buffer state to protect the system of African American and African enslavement in South Carolina.

75.   1738—Smallpox epidemic. Cherokee smallpox was often caused by Europeans giving Indians blankets that were used by smallpox disease-stricken Europeans.

76.   1739—The first freedom march in America. On September 9, 1739, Gullah people fought for their freedom during a "Freedom War" in Charleston. They marched to St. Augustine,

Gullah attack upon plantation owners (enslavers)

Florida. There were freedom wars fought by Gullahs against enslavers, including the Stono River Revolt, led by Cato.

77. 1739—Gullahs launched a series of attacks on planters that caused them to stop importing Africans for ten years.

78. 1740—First state highway patrol unofficially organized to enforce the cruel Slave Codes of 1740.

79. 1742—Gambian Africans in Africa attacked and destroyed the slaver ship, the "Mary Galley," which was destined for the Sea Islands of America.

80. 1745—Gullahs harvested 104,680 barrels of rice, enough rice for American consumption and to export to the Mediterranean (yielded higher profits).

81. 1745—Texas invaded and violently taken from Native Americans. Many Gullahs lived in Texas at that time.

82.   1748—First chemistry teachers in America. Eliza Lucas Pinckney was taught indigo extraction and color stabilization by Gullah textile craftsman.

83.   1750—Gullah slave shipyard called Bouncie Island, in the Sierra Leone River, was used as a slave shipyard by the English. They sold directly to Charleston, South Carolina. These slaves were highly educated and skilled.

84.   1755—South Carolina Provincial Legislature passed a law to keep Blacks with advanced technological knowledge out of trades. The Blacks far outnumbered whites in trades and skills during this time.

85.   1763—The "Franciscan Mercenary and Missionary Technique" also called the "Bible or the Bullet," was first used on the Yemassee, and later on the Gullah. This same technique was later used on Native Americans in Texas to steal land and to murder.

86.   1764—Gullah slave-labor gives England enormous wealth. All the cotton from the American colonies had to be shipped to the colonial power, and then it was sold. This process allowed England to gain huge profits from Gullah slave-labor.

87.   1774—Gullah slaves, no money down. Credit plan for purchase of slaves. After the American Revolution, the British continued to collect taxes in American territory they controlled and in an effort to get rid of Gullah and Indian slaves, sold them on credit. Sometimes one-fourth to one-half down with payment plans.

88.   1775—Lacrosse was first played in America. This game was introduced to whites in the Sea Island area by the Cherokee people.

89.   1776—The original version of the Declaration of Independence gave African American captives their freedom. The Sea Islands' state representatives opposed this version, and had any references to freeing African Americans omitted from the document.

90.   1784—Sea Islands' cotton increased the wealth of the South and saved the South from economic depression. Later in history, chemist George Washington Carver's products from the bean called the peanut caused the peanut and soy beans to economically save the South from another depression.

91.   1788—Gullahs were the first African Americans to found a city in Africa. Freetown, Sierra Leone, the Capital, is the city they established.

92.   1788—First African American descendants of Sierra Leone to move back to that country were Gullahs.

93.   1790—Gullah organization founded to maintain schools for children. The Brown Fellowship Society was founded in Charleston, South Carolina for educational matters affecting African Americans.

94.   1800—The largest U.S. export to the Mediterranean countries was Sea Islands' rice.

95.   1800—Mulatto (light-skinned) Gullah's slavery businesses were ruined by a Haitian. The Haitian Revolution, led by Toussaint

L'Ouverture ruined the slavery business of Mulattoes. Mulatto ownership of other African Americans was created by whites to show moral justification of slavery. Many "free" African Americans bought the freedom of their parents and other relatives, and thus technically were classified as "slave owners" by whites.

96. **1800** (circa)—The last shipment of Gullah captives (slaves) arrived in the Sea Islands. The ship landed at Sand Island, which is an island between Hardeeville and Ridgeland, South Carolina. The bell of the ship is in the tower of Hardeeville Methodist Church.

97. **1800**—African Americans to demonstrate bravery in battle. "The Port Royal Experiment" was a test to show how bravely Blacks could defend the whites in the Sea Islands.

98. **1800**—Black U.S. soldiers to be lynched by white Americans. After the Black Militia was organized to enforce marshall law and protect the North's capture of Southern territory, white vigilantes, militia and mobs lynched many of these men, often while wearing their army uniforms.

99. **1800**—Race riots. Gullah homes were burned and people were murdered because of the Black Militia's presence.

100. **1800**—First African American state. During this time, 80 percent of the population of South Carolina was African American.

101. **1800**—The highest point in South Carolina was given a name derived from the African language, Sassa. The point is called Sassafras

Bloodhounds and hunters attacking a family of fugitive
slaves: "nigger dogs" were trained to help capture runaways
(Courtesy of the Library of Congress)

Mountain. Sassafras is also the name of an
herb once used to treat syphilis.

102.   1800—The stopping of a funeral procession
at the cemetery gate. This was done to gain
spiritual permission to enter the spirit world
(graveyard).

103.   1800—First totally independent African
American communities were established.
"Runaway Slave" (Africans seeking freedom)
communities were established by Gullahs
from the Sea-Islands. They were found in
northern Florida, lower Alabama, and
Tennessee. The Spanish called these Africans
"Seminoles," which is Spanish for "Cameroon,"
which means runaway in French.

104.   1800—Negro spiritual, "Swing Low, Sweet
Harriet," sang to indicate escape via underground railroad. Gullah plans to escape were

communicated in "time," "place," and "event" cryptic code of gospels when whites were around. The gospel songs and words were often changed to "Swing Low, Sweet Chariot" when whites were near. Today, it is sung as "Sing Low, Sweet Chariot."

105. 1800—Morris Code. The African drum rhythm language was stolen and renamed the Morris Code. A type of electrical pulse rhythm is used by telephones, television, computers, and radios, which is converted to words and/or pictures. Rhythm language was used by Gullahs to communicate secret messages. Gullah fisherman used drum language to call Dolphins and get them to herd fish to their nets. Gullah ladies would send messages by beating on wash tubs or pounding scrub boards.

106. 1812—Gullahs attacked by Andrew Jackson. General Jackson used the War of 1812 as an excuse to attack and murder the Gullahs in communities in Florida and lower Alabama.

107. 1812—African myths, used by Gullahs, were called "tall tales" and some were published by David Crockett. The origins of these myths are found in the book, *Coming Forth by Day*, (so-called Egyptian Book of the Dead) written before 1500 B.C.

108. 1812—American marines were defeated by Gullahs and American Indians in Florida (first Seminole wars).

109. 1817—First and largest free African American church was formed. This was the African Methodist Episcopal Church in Charleston, South Carolina. It was one of the only Black Churches closed by the govern-

ment for starting rebellions. It mixed Africanisms and Maat (reciprocity, reparations, etc.) with Christianity.

110. 1820—A Sea Islands' planter owned the last ship that carried "slave cargo" to America. The ship was called the "Wanderer."

111. 1820—First anti-slavery magazine was published in a Sea Islands state. The magazine was called *The Emancipator*.

112. 1822— "Gullah Jack" was Denmark Vesy's Commander of the Army. He was born in Angola, Africa.

113. 1822—Denmark Vesy led the first recorded major revolt by the Gullahs. Africans attacked and fought Europeans (Swedish, Danes, Portuguese, Russians, etc.) that invaded Africa for slaves, fought on slaves' ships, and attacked slave ships constantly during slavery. They fought Europeans from

Runaway slaves formed independent communities
(MK)

all major religions (Christians, Jews, Moslems), as well as occult groups (Satan Worshipers).

114. 1822—Elijah McCoy invented the self-lubricating device that is used in cars, trains, planes, spaceships and machines. Whites who wanted to know if an engine was self-lubricating would ask, "Is it the Real McCoy?" Elijah McCoy's mother was a Gullah lady.

115. 1830—Largest indigo farms in America harvested by the Gullahs.

116. 1834—Law passed that it is illegal to educate free Negroes and slaves. This was caused by Denmark Vesey and Nat Turner revolts. The whites feared educated African Americans would seek justice through any means.

117. 1842—The Gullah and other runaway slaves were the first African Americans, in history, that the U.S. declared war against. "The Negro War" was declared by General Jesup. He informed the War Department that runaway Gullahs were able and willing to try to defeat the U.S.A. In 1842, the U.S. Army attacked and defeated the runaway Gullah communities and marched them at gunpoint to Oklahoma.

118. 1850—First African American reservation. Gullahs and other slaves from "runaway slave" communities were chased by U.S. soldiers across Texas into Mexico, where reservation-type settlements existed for African Americans.

119. 1850—Texas Rangers were an official Band that attacked Gullahs in Texas. These Gullahs were being chased out of the Carolinas through Florida, through New Orleans, through Texas, and eventually ended up in Mexico. West African languages accents, Congo words and African word order are noted in these states since that date.

120. 1855 (circa)— "Brick" Baptist Church built because Beaufort Baptist Church had 156 whites and 3,557 Blacks. The whites built the original Brick Church so they could worship God properly (segregated, "whites only").

121. 1858—First aid station/hospital. Aminta (Harriet Tubman) worked for the European

(white) Underground Railroad on Port Royal Island. Slave rebels, women and children first created escape hideouts and routes called the Underground Railroad. White businessmen politically sponsored their own railroad to weaken their business opponents and the South by stealing their slave labor supply. Slave owners, in order to increase their plantation profits would use the underground railroad as a way to do slave rustling in their opponents slaves. Freeing the slaves was not their concern as they believed Drapetomania existed. Drapetomania is the mental illness that causes a slave to runaway. They used Harriet Tubman and erroneously take sole credit for the development of the underground railroad.

122.   1859-1931—During this time, the largest U.S. stock investment was in the enslavement of the Africans. The U.S. invested two-billion dollars in slavery. This was twice the amount spent on railroads. Seventy percent of its foreign trade was from cotton. The most expensive and the most wanted cotton was Sea Islands cotton. This cotton produced more revenue and sold for two to ten times the price of regular cotton.

123.   1860—Whites segregated their congregations by making the Gullahs sit in the so-called "Nigger Sections."

124.   1860—Twelve percent of Indian territory was occupied by the Gullahs and other African Americans.

125.   1860—The Sea Islands Secession Act. Edisto Island was the first island to secede from the Union.

126. 1861—Gullah and other slaves who escaped slavery in the South and moved to Northern states were subjected to twice as much White Racism. They were treated badly by the racist Abolitionists who believed Negroes to be inferior. Many Northern states had slaves (i.e., New York, Delaware, Rhode Island, etc.). The ex-slaves' treatment in the North was so horrible that they would sing the song, *I Wish I Was in Dixie.*

127. 1861—On "Civil War Day" or "Gun Shoot Day," whites left the islands. "Gun Shoot" is the Gullah name for the Union defeat of the Confederate Army. Whites abandoned the islands on this day, leaving the Blacks as the only inhabitants. The Union Army did not free the slaves. The Emancipation Proclamation did not free slaves and allowed states to continue to have slaves. The Confederate Government and British emancipated slaves before Lincoln. The 13th Amendment was passed eight months after Abraham Lincoln's death. It ended chattel captivity (chained slavery) but did not end captivity (unchained slavery). It illegally made ex-slaves U.S. citizens and took away their Human Rights and gave them Civil Rights (Slave's Rights). Emancipated slaves could be fined for so-called illegal behavior. If unable to pay the fine, they would have to work six months without pay for the state or a private business or white citizen. This was worse than slavery.

128. 1862—The Penn School started as an educational experiment by Ellen Murry and Laura Towne in Oaks Plantation. William Penn designed the school for the domestication of the Gullahs. Despite his reputation as a fair and just "friend," Penn proved to be a bigot.

John Jefferson, a Black Seminole (Indigeneous African
American) enlisted in the 10th U.S. Cavalry

He designed separate pews for Blacks and
whites. He stole land from Native Americans,
and in Pennsylvania, he condemned a woman
to death allegedly for being a witch.

129.   1862—Black military organized during the
Civil War. General Saxton was allowed to
accept up to 5,000 African American volun-
teers (this was similar to the military quotas
still in use today).

130. 1862—Harriet Tubman's basket name (African) was Aminta. She baked goods for the Confederates in a house on Port Republic and Charles Streets. Harriet Tubman was a functional title given to many women who helped free slaves.

131. 1863—First strike by U.S. Army soldiers. Gullah and other Black soldiers refused to accept pay until they were paid the same rate as white Union solders. The strike lasted 18 months. Blacks were paid $7.00 a month, while whites were paid $13.00.

132. 1863—Congressional Medal of Honor winners. Three Gullahs, who were erroneously called "Seminole Negro Indian Scouts," won the medals of honor.

133. 1863—Gullah U.S. military regiment freed Black captives. On June 3, 1863, Harriet Tubman and 250 armed Black soldiers of the 2nd Regiment led 727 captives to freedom.

134. 1863—Tabernacle Baptist Church was organized. Many African American churches in Beaufort had their origin at Tabernacle. A bust of General Robert Smalls is located there.

135. 1864—A savings bank for Sea Islands' Gullahs was established by General Rufus Saxon. Gullahs deposited more than $240,000, and were swindled out of their savings by the U.S. Government and Saxon.

136. 1864—United States Colored Troops deposited $55,000 in the Freedman's Savings Bank of Beaufort. They used the money to purchase Sea Islands property.

137. 1864—U.S. Government gave Sea Islands to Gullahs. General William T. Sherman issued Field Order Number 15, which designated that the Sea Islands and 30 miles inland from Charleston, South Carolina, be given to the Gullahs. President Johnson changed that order four months later, and the Gullahs ended up with much less territory.

138. 1865—First African American Secretary of State and State Treasurer, Francis L. Cardozo.

139. 1865—First African American Lieutenant Governor of a state was Alonzo J. Ransier of South Carolina.

140. 1866—One of the first fire departments for a city with all African Americans. Gullahs formed fire companies, the Vigilant and Enterprise Company.

141. 1867—The first African American school board for a major public school system was on Port Royal Island (Commonly referred to as Beaufort). The Africans pattern it after The Council of the Elders/Wise. Being an Elder/Wise is a function. Therefore, a 30-year-old adult could be classified as an Elder. Former slaves used the African educational structure to start the first public schools in the Carolinas.

142. 1867—Beaufort County School Board was composed exclusively of African Americans: I.J. Cohen, Richard H. Gleaves, R.F. Bythewood, Walter Fuller, Landon S. Langley, Isaac Simmons, J.C. Rivers, Prince Rivers, Robert Smalls, Arthur Waddell, George Waddell, William Whipper, and Jonathan Wright.

143.   1859-68—First deep sea divers in America. Gullah divers dived for phosphorous matter from an underwater fossil river 10 to 30 miles from the Wando River, south to the Broad River. This phosphate was used as a fertilizer for plantation crops.

144.   1861-70—Black U.S. Army troops used to put whites under martial law in Southern States in America. The Black Militia of 70,000 was the largest group of armed African Americans in America.

145.   1861-70—Most influential newspaper in the African American communities of the South, *The Missionary Record*, was published in South Carolina by Richard H. "Daddy" Cain.

146.   1861-7— "The Gullah Statesman," Robert Smalls held state office for six years and served five terms in the U.S. Congress. He and his crew of men, women and children captured a confederate steamer (The Planter) and gave it to the Union Army during the Civil War. A bust of Mr. Smalls is at the Tabernacle Baptist Church in Beaufort, South Carolina.

147.   1861-70—Senator John C. Calhoun issued a warning that South Carolina would become Africanized. Added to this, African King Menelik gave several million dollars in gold to the United States to be given to exslaves. Senator Thaddeus Stevens made the reparational promise to give each Negro "40 acres and a mule," which is currently equal to more than $300,000. The Government stole the gold and put it in Fort Knox and has never given the gold or profit from interest to African Americans.

148.   1861-70—Famous African American politicians of the Sea Islands area were Jonathan Jasper Wright, a member of the South Carolina Supreme Court for seven years and Robert Elliott, who served in the U.S. Congress and the South Carolina Legislature.

149.   1861-70—Largest cotton press in the world was in Port Royal.

150.   1861-70—One of the first Black historians was a Sea Islands resident named Martin R. Delaney. He was also an African explorer and an agent for the Freedman's Bureau.

151.   1861-70—Railroad coaches manufactured on Port Royal Island with Gullah laborers.

152.   1874—Father Divine (1874-1965) was born on the Gullah Sea Island of Hutchinson Island, Georgia. He was a famous religious leader who used strict moral and social rules as part of his teachings (no smoking, drinking, or cosmetics).

153.   1877—First all-African American National Guard type unit. The Black Militia (consisted mostly of Gullahs).

154.   1881—Dr. York W. Bailey, first Gullah medical doctor. Bailey was born on St. Helena Island. He used herbs and traditional medicine to help his patients.

155.   1883—Shoemaking machine invented by African American, Jan E. Matzeliger. His mother was from West Africa (Rice Coast Gullahs).

156. 1887—Marcus Mosiah Garvey (1887-1940) created an international economic and social movement. He was born on the island of Jamaica, where Gullah people were tortured until they accepted slavery. His slogans were "Africa for Africans," and "One God, One Aim, One Destiny." He started the use of the colors red, black and green on the African American flag.

157. 1887—V. H. James was born in Carolina. He organized the first art gallery that was controlled and directed by African Americans (at Howard University).

158. 1889—Gullahs had four units that fought the Spanish-American war. Gullah soldiers that rode with Teddy Roosevelt's "Rough Riders" were given a dishonorable discharge on a claim that they raped a white woman. In 1980, it was changed to an honorable discharge.

159. 1891—First demand by African Americans for reparations (back wages). Gullah Congress-man, Thomas E. Miller, asked that plantation checks issued to Gullahs by whites be honored by the state.

160. 1900—Gullah music made popular in America. George Gershwin copied Gullah music and composed the musical, *Porgy and Bess.* He studied the Gullah music in Charleston and traveled to the Islands to steal the authentic sounds, rhythms, and copyright them. He and many other white musicians continuously get paid royalty money for the music and reworded songs stolen from Africans born in America.

161.   1900—The song, *Michael Row De Boat
Ashore,* was copied by missionaries from the
Gullah boatmen that sang it as they worked
on the ferry boats in downtown Beaufort
(Carteret and Bay Streets).

162.   1910—Gullah race riot was on May 2, 1910
on St. Helena Island. Gullahs attacked,
wounded and killed one United States Army
soldier at Fort Freemont, off Land's End
Road. The United States Government failed
to prosecute or jail any Blacks involved as
white racism obviously caused the incident.
The newspaper failed to explain the incident
beyond it being a social evening that erupted
in violence.

163.   1926—First cotton fabric used to pave a road.
Cotton Road was paved in Chapin County,
South Carolina.

164.   1932—The George Washington quarter (25
cents) had a picture of an eagle on one side.
George Washington owned, raped, and mur-
dered slaves. He is considered a criminal.
Henry William DeSaussure (owner of the
Gold Eagle Hotel on New Street near Bay
Street) designed the eagle. It is the African
symbol of Isis and Maat.

165.   1986—The National Gullah Festival was for-
mally organized by Rosalie Pazant and her
daughters, Lolita, Charlotte, and Reba. The
Festival educates African Americans and
other Americans about Gullah history, heritage, and lifestyle.

SLAVE REVOLT AFFIRMATION

During slavery/colonialism, the Africans on the Continent and Diaspora (i.e., Gullah) would secretly meet in the bush or cabins to tell African folktales and/or perform Maatian (Theme of justice, harmony, reciprocity, etc.) rituals and ceremonies. They would organize military counterattacks (rebellions) against the Europeans. Many chants of encouragement and positive affirmations were recited in order to keep the spirit of freedom, statesmanship, and military consciousness alive. The militant slave men, women, and children understood that without a military to protect them and attack their European (American Whites) enemies, freedom cannot and will not exist.

The following are a few examples of affirmations.

Du Free-dum	*Freedom is ours*
E knot de tongue	*I promise*
Du Free-dum	*Freedom is ours*
Fuhr ride de buckra frame	*To fight the Whites*
Uh tek back de tief um	*And, take back all that they stole from us*

Du Free-dum	*Freedom is ours*
Ef e no do um Gawd tek e soul	*If I don't may I die =* *God take my soul*

Du Free-dum.	*Freedom is ours.*
Fuhr tru.	*It is true.*
Du Free-dum.	*Freedom is ours.*

(Swahili)

Eh! Eh! Bomba! Heu! Heu!	*We swear to defeat* *(destroy)*
Canga, bafia te Canga, moune de le	*The Whites and all that* *they possess*
Conga, do ki la	*Let us die rather than*
Congo, li	*Fail to keep this vow*

A 19th-century African Spiritual Dance usually accompanied
meetings about counter-attacks on whites
(Drawing by E.W. Kemble. Courtesy of the New York Public Library)

How to Speak
Conversational Gullah

The Gullah conversational language, like all African languages is organic (living). Gullah is alive, constantly changing and can be improvised upon. It really is rapping in the African tongue. In speaking Gullah, you should mix and match sentences and words from these conversations in order to communicate. The purpose of language is to communicate not to be grammatically correct. Language reflects the current and past history of a people. The sounds and rhythms of the words will lead you to good combinations. The more you speak it, the better. These are just a few Gullah sentences and words that you can use to get started on your cultural journey.

CONBESATE

Yello
Wuh do um? or Wuh Fuhr do?
Wuh ya name?
Me name yiz...
Who e yiz?
Me name yiz...,
Glad fuh saa'b yah.

CONVERSATION

Hello.
How are you?
What is your name?
My name is...
Who are you?
My name is...
I am glad to meet you.

The Gullah

E too glan fuh see yah — I am glad to see/meet you also.

Yuh duh talk en Gullah? — **Can you speak Gullah?**
Uh ent nebbuh crack me teet fuhr Gullah much. — I cannot speak much Gullah.
Wuh ya gwi do? — **What are you going to do?**

Wuh e wan? — What do you want to do?
Lea fuh *fess-tibble, kar, hoe-tell* — **Go directly to the *festival, car, hotel*.**
Ya fuh gone? — Are you going?
Uh gwine *tuhmorroh, day clean.* — I am going *tomorrow, today.*

E uh fine day. — **It is a nice day.**
E yiz fuh tru — Yes, it is.
Un tie e mout — **Let's talk.**
Uh binnah talk — I've been talking.
Uh mos dead wid de loansum — **I've been by myself.**
Wuh ya duh talk bout? — What do you want to talk about?

De Gullah Fess-tibble — **The Gullah Festival**
Yeddy me? — **Did you hear me?**
Uh nebbuh yeddy — I did not hear you.
Uh yent sub uh kin fin num *fess-tibble, kar, hoe-tell, etc.* — I cannot find the *festival, car, hotel.*
E obuh yanduh — **It s/he is over there.**
Tengk ya — **Thank you**
Berry Welden — **You are very welcome**
Gib de time uh day? — What time is it?
Cal um seben de clock — It is seven o'clock
Wuh de time be done bruk-up? — **What time is it over?**
Uh lee — Early.
Nuf peeple bunch-up innar — **There are many people there.**

Cu leh wez gwine — **Come, let's go.**
Uh gwine set een de cheer — I am going to sit in this chair.

Uh waa'k til uh agonize me bone — I walked until I am exhausted.
E onduhstan — **I (s/he) understand**

48

E hab plaz ene haa't	**I have a place in my heart for you.**
Bimeby un gwine de *fess-tibble, hotel, etc.*	After awhile, I am going to the *festival, hotel, etc.*
E a mout dry up	**You, I, s/he stopped talking.**
Uh gwine lick back en yah kin crack ya teet	I will come back and talk

USEFUL SENTENCES

E gone bedout e mek e mannus	S/he left without saying goodbye.
Uh yeh hab cajun fuh meet um	I am glad to meet you.
E posit e wud	S/he didn't say a word
De compuh say long um	S/he talks a long time
E mek de long tark	S/he gossips
E bex long e mout	S/he used cursing
Dat beat me time	I can't believe it
It ah sickenin ting	It is worrisome
E paw tun puss'n	S/he is an important person
Den cun fuh shum	They come to see her/him
Uh spon d uh yent know un	They act like they don't know *me, us, you.*
E cheap um yah	S/he insulted you
E ain't hab all de buttons	S/he does not have good sense
Pay um no min	Ignore *them, her, him, it.*
E bow dashus	S/he is bold
E projic wid um	S/he interferes.
E dribuh fus news	You drive next.
Yah dribuh duh two time.	You drive twice.
Wuh de mout box up?	Why are you frowning?
Oonuh suck e teet.	You disagree
Lee ax um	I asked.
Yah no fuhr always eet out de same spoon.	We don't always agree.
Uh gwine tuhreckly.	I am leaving soon.
E dunk yuh.	I don't care.

Wich pussun b'long un?	Which person does this belong to?
E gon spang.	Go quickly.
Shut de do e *car, room, etc.*	Close the *car, room, etc.* door .
Tengky fuhr eberyting e cum lick back.	Thanks for everything. I will come back.
Me gwine.	I am going.
Wen fuhr las time e fuhr see yah?	When was the last time I saw you?
E no fuhr memba.	I don't remember.
Cudda layed yee onna yah enna Augus, Septemba, Actowba?	It could have been August, September, October.
E tangledy lee haad.	I am confused.
Ub benna swim longso e noh swim moe.	I swam so long I could not swim any more.
Oonuh tek dem pic-char?	You take our picture?
Wuh de camarah.	Hold the camera.
Move yuh haad/esef dat way.	Move your head/yourself that way.
Tap yah su.	Stop there.
Mek teet shwo ye tuh yez.	Smile.
Mek wen yah reddee.	Tell me when you are ready.
Uh ben spen me time onnah beech.	I spent all my time at the beach.
Uuh tote le towil wid yuh?	Did you take a towel with you?

GOING OUT TO EAT

Dey done git bittle/food.	**Let's go and eat.**
E belly pinch um.	S/he is hungry
Gi we som bittle.	**Give me some food.**
Ennybody gwine wid me?	**Anybody going with me.**
Yuh fuhr gwine?	**Are you going?**
Uh hab moanee fuh bittle/food?	**I have money for food.**
Uh done fuh eetin de day.	**I have already eaten.**
Uh hab nut eet.	I have not eaten.

50

Uh hab moanee fuh bittle/food?	**I have money for food.**
Uh done fuh eetin de day.	**I have already eaten.**
Uh hab nut eet.	I have not eaten.
Dey ent hab nutt n fuh eet.	I/we did not have anything to eat.
E brakfus eet?	Did you eat breakfast?
Un ben reddee fuh *brakfus, dinnah, etc.*	**I am ready for** *breakfust, dinner, etc.*
Fallaw me tudda ress-runt.	Follow me to the restaurant.
E kant wait.	I cannot wait.
Lukkuh dat pussu pack up de mout.	Look at that person stuff themselves.
E wah nuff bittle.	I want plenty to eat.
Dese caffee bun pon e mout lips.	**The coffee burns my lips.**
Yuh bittle/foo nayam betta ter fuhr ussum.	**Your food tasts bet than ours.**
Gi e ah lilli moe bittle.	Give me more to eat.
E blang time wait ponde bittle.	**I have waited a long time for food.**
Wuh dem peeple de nyam?	What are those people eating?
De chillun/chile n yam.	**The children/child have/has eaten.**
Uh know wuffuh done eet.	I don't know what to eat.
Uh study e head.	**You think about it.**
Wuh e wan eet?	What do you want to eat?
Oonuh hab swit toot	**You like sweets**
E wan tas'e' mout bittle/foot.	I want something good to eat.
E gwine tuh gedduh fuhr de ress-runt.	**Let's go to the restaurant.**
Wuffuh ress-runt kin chuss wuh yah?	Which restaurant should we choose?
No, uh yent fuh go de ress-runt	**I do not know which restaurant to go to.**
Ef e gwine pay fuhr um?	Are you going to pay?

Uh anduddah wu'se done pay. Fuh tru.	**I will pay another day. That's the truth.**
Dem gwine fuh bye bittle.	S/he is going to buy the food.
Cum leh we gon.	Let's go.
Uh gwine set een eeet.	**I am going to sit and eat.**
Bress de bittle.	Bless the food.
Tek e pledjuh de bittle.	**Enjoy your food.**
Pledjuh e sefe.	**Enjoy our self.**
Uh eet mawn.	I want to eat more.
Bittle wen et lib fuhr.	**Food is all you live for.**
Id tas lik sum moe.	It tastes good.
Fuh satify fuhr trute.	**I am satisfied.**
E tummach bittle fuh eat.	S/he ate too much.
Enybody wuh tote de bittle tuh dem?	**Anybody want to take food to the others?**
Dem gwine fuh bye bittle.	They, s/he will buy food.
How long e stan so?	**How long have we been here?**
E yent figguh fuh go.	I don't know.
E mek ansuh suh e yent d-um.	**I do not know the answer.**
Come leh we gwine.	**Let's go.**

TRAVEL

Mek fuh!	Go!
Co'se uh gwine.	Of course, I am going.
Wuh long mout um?	Why are you pouting?
Le'm.	Let *them, her, him, etc.*
E one ob we people.	S/he is one of us.
We se'f gwin.	We will go with you.*Or* We went ourselves.
E swit mout fren.	S/he is a good friend.
Mek mout um yez tuh yez.	Smile.
Lick back gwine wid yah de *kar, hoe-tell, fess-tibble.*	We will go back with you to the *car, hotel, festival, etc.*
E look lukkuh anuddah puss'un.	*S/he, it* looks like someone else.
Ya fictive?	Are you kinfolk/related?
E bu out wid de laugh.	S/he laughed.

E full up nice un up.	S/he is full of flattering talk.
Wuh ya knot ya face?	Why are you frowning?
Cu leh we gwine.	Come, let's go.
Yah gwine bidout um.	You go without me.
Yah cyan leenfuh um.	You can leave without *me, them, etc.*
Uh waa gone de *hoe-tell, kar, fess-tible,* etc.	I want to go to the *hotel, car, festival, etc.*
How dem kin lik back de *hoe-tell, kar,* etc.	How can I get back to the *hotel, car,* etc.
E need fuh gon back tuh de...	*I need to go back to the...*
Lick back gwine.	Turn around and go.
E gwine pon de tour.	I am going on the tour.
Oonuh hab in-gin sic.	You have engine problems?
E affen rent ah kar.	I want to rent a car.
Ho mucha mile fra yah beef'ut?	How many miles to Beaufort?
E yent gwine de *Beef'ut, kar, fess-tibble,* etc.	I am going to *Beaufort, car, festival,* etc.
Uh gwine.	I am going.
Uh yeddy um.	I am ready.
Uh yen know w'eddub don gwine?	I don't know whether they are going.
Yah dribuh de kar	You drive the car.
Yah dribuh fus gwine	You drive first.

CHILLUM TALK	**CHILDREN TALK**
Mek so de chillum/? chile gone	Where are/is the children/child?
Uh yent shum.	I did not see them.
De chillum dem gone.	The children have left.
Gone at fuhr um.	Go after them.
Uh shum.	I see them.
De chillum/chile gone fuh shum gen.	The children/child are/is gone again.
Dem beat du't tun.	They ran as fast as s/he could.
Weh e iz?	Where is/are *s/he, they?*

The Gullah

E yent dey.

S/he, they were/was not there.

Light out fuhr um.

Go after them.

PARENT/CHILD CONVERSATE

Weh e be gwine?
Ub bin saach fuhr.

Where were you?
I have been looking for you.

Wuh e do?

What have you been doing?

De wadde plash all obub um.

The water splashed all over me.

Bex, long e ye ye.
Nebbuh hapee no mo.
Ef id ben wusser,
Ah be most dead.
E cum fuh see yah cus e tangledy.

I was so angry I cried.
I was unhappy.
If it was worse, I would have died (drown).
I came to see you because I was confused.

Uh yent shum yah.
Ah went fuhr play til dry.

I did not see you.
So, I went to play until I got dry.

De boduhr um tummuch.
Yah no wiffud me do?
Ah know ya befo e bawn.
Fuhr trute. Naw wha tek ya long so.
E choir fuh liss'ne.

It bothered me so much.
You know what I'll do?
I know you well. Now, tell me what took you so long.
I will be quiet and listen.

CHILLUM WUDS

Dem chillum/chile berry bejun.

CHILDREN WORDS

The children/child are/is very obedient.

De chillum/chile behave too bad.

The children/child behaved badly.

De chile los e parents.

The child lost its parents.

De chillum/chile too stiff.

The children/child are/is impatient.

54

De chile know wud how
  fuhr drop legs.

That child is a good
  dancer.

De da-ance tillum feet
  batam burn.

They danced a long time.

Weh e dey left dem cry.

When I left they cried.

Nyung chillum lub fuhr *play*,
sing, dance, etc.

The children love to *play*,
  sing, dance, etc.

Git way fum ya.

Get away from there.

Gedduh tuh de paa'k.

Gather in the park.

Uh ack sident bin hab.

There was an accident.

Yuh un es.

Here I am.

Man chile

Boy

Ooman chile.

Girl

Piss tail chile.

Child that wets on
  themselves, childish
  teenager, or immature
  person.

SHOPPING

Wuh cum fuh see?

What are you looking for?

Wuh e wan?

What do you want?

Unrabble de mout.

Talk about it.

E cum fuh see closes.

I want to see clothes.

Pick wuh ya chose.

Select what you want.

Wuh dat iz?

What is it?

Wuh ya duh shop fuh?

What are you shopping for?

Ub bin saa ch uh fuhr.

I have been looking for . . . .

E uh berry soon *ooman,
man, pussun.*

I am a stylish (classy)
  woman, man, person.

E tukkuh.

It is similar.

Uh no fuh do um.

Don't do it (buy it).

E sane lukkuh.

It looks the same.

Trau c ye ye.

Look closely.

E de cyan specify e yen wu't.

It looks worthless.

Uh bye um fum yanduh.

Buy another place.

Dat cos tummach.

It cost too much.

W'en ya com de fuhr deal,
  e mus know fuhr deal.

When you look for a bargain
  you must know a bargain.

E chance um.

Take a risk. Risk it.

The Gullah

Luk onduh neet dat.
Look underneath that.

Wuh e suh?
What did you see?

Yah tangledy.
I am confused.

Hep me wid dese.
Help me with this.

E suh de cost?
What is the price?

Wuh e wort?
What is it worth?

Do um.
Do it. Buy it.

Uh sho ent wan lef til bye um.
I am not going until I buy it.

Yah tiefin de ting.
You are getting it at a steal. *Or* It is a cheap price.

Fuh worree nun.
Don't worry.

E suck e teet.
I disagree.

Us spen all de dolluh tuh de *sto, fess-tibble, etc.*
We spent all my money at the *store, festival, etc.*

E gwine fuhr bye de ting?
Are you going to buy the thing?

Shop, been weh e lib fuhr.
Shopping is what I live for.

Ah wan fuhr pay.
I want to pay for it.

Uh en fuh credik cha'age um.
I want to charge it on my credit card.

Oonuh pleez, kin gimme fuhr change.
May I have change.

E bye tummach tings.
You buy too many things.

Un mus min e bidness.
You mind your own business.

Yah gone bye towing jisso.
You buy for no particular reason.

E haa'dly kin spen.
You hardly can pay for it.

E bin dry long so e spen.
It's been a long time since I have spent money.

Cyan no tel yah enne ting.
I cannot tell you anything.

Ef e bi dis oonuh no kan bi dat.
If you buy this, you cannot buy that.

E mek leh walk roun little fus.
Let me walk around a little first.

De cos yiz bettar obah dese.
The price is better over there.

Mek leh try obad de
Let's try over there at that

56

plaz, sto, etc.	*place, store, etc.*
E nuh want des sum.	I don't want it.
Tekkah lee dollah offah	Take off a dollar and
e buy um.	I will buy it.
Wea de price drap e	When the price drops, I will
lick back.	return.
WEDDUH	WEATHER
Dat rain uh day clean.	It is raining today.
Yass, e dun rain haad.	Yes, it is really raining
Fuhr trute.	hard.
E duh wedduh.	It is storming.
Yuh fuhr gwine?	Are you going?
Pen pun on de wedduh.	It depends on the weather.
E too daa'k fuhr dem go.	It's too dark to go.
Dem cand'l lite n.	It's night time.
E...	It is...
...nigh um	...night
...fuss–daa'k	...evening
...so–lean	...sundown
E uh fine day.	It is a nice day.
Tuhmorruh uh fine day.	Tomorrow will be a nice day.
E uh-ly.	It is early.

	HEALTH	
E yent hel tee.		I am healthy
E yent sic.		I am sick.
De flam graff e haad.		I have a head cold.
De col e hab um.		I have a cold.
E he'th stan po.		You look sick.
Dey bin sick.		They are sick.
E sugar got me.		I have diabetes.
Uh gwine all do uh		I am going although I don't
feel sowtuh so.		feel like it.
De misery bin hab um.		I don't feel well.
Yah aggabate tummach.		You worry too much.
De ritis agonize me bone.		I have arthritis.
E nature gwine.		I have a *sex problem,*
		impotence, frigidity.

The Gullah

Me teet hab hurten een agga-bate.	I have a tooth ache.
Ub ben feel likkah yiz gonna drap sic.	I feel like I am getting sick.
E hab lee blood presha.	I have high blood pressure.
Don't press me nerves.	Don't stress me.
Oonuh helf cud-dah betta do-um.	Your health could be better.
Yuh haben fus aid kit?	Do you have a first aid kit?
Lee horse-biddle tek pleez.	Take me to the hospital.

USEFUL WORDS

Aa'm	hands
Adduh'res	others
Bekase	because
Bex tek um	angry
Buckra	white person
Cum fuh	come
Crab crack	eat crabs
Dig dut	ran
De bey graff	grab
Ent	is / are / does / did
Else so	otherwise
En	and
En ting	other things
E stan	It is so
E	he, she, it
Fr'en	friend
Fus	first
Flam	phlegm, mucus, cold, sinus
Greese e mout	taste good
Gree	agree
Lee	the
Low	admit
Light out	go after
Likeso	also
Min um	take care of it, him
Nyam	to eat
Oonuh	you
Ooman	woman

58

Paa'k	park
Papuh	paper
Peruse	slowly
Pun top	on top
Pit	put
Pussun	person
Rid e frame	fight
Ramify rawn	rude, unmannerly
Sugar num	without
Tief	steal
Ye ye	eye

Shu, the god of the atmosphere, seated on the sign for gold. A carving on the back of one of the elaborate royal chairs from the tomb of Tutankhamon. Eighteenth Dynasty. Egyptian Museum, Cairo.

GULLAH PROVERBS

A pound of mouth shut, worth ounce explainin'.

Promisin talk don cook rice.

Det wan ditch you arn fuh jump.
Death is one ditch you have to jump.

Ebery day ya tote lee buckit tuh de well in disa dey
de bottam he gwine drop outta.
*Every day one takes chances, but one
day your luck will run out.*

Empty sack can't sand upright alone.

Ef you hol you made e would kill e by glad.
*If you hold your anger it will kill
all your happiness.*

Er good run bettuh dan uh bad stan.
A good run is better than a bad stand.

E by back is fitted to de bu'den.
Every person is able to carry his own burden.

The Gullah

Heart don't mean every thing mough say.

Sin is easier to stand dan shame.

Sad we got to be burn fore we learn.

Still water gits stale an scummy too quick.
It can wash away sin.
*Don't wait too long to apologize because it will be
stale, but it still is an apology.*

Tit fuh tat, but tar fuh fat, et yuh.

Kill my dawg, I kill yuh cat.
For every action, there is an equal reaction.

Trouble goin fall! Ain't goin fall on da ground!
Goin fall on somebody.

Mo rain, mo ress, but fair wedder bin bess.

Onpossible *(impossible)* ta git straight
wud from crooker timber.

Most hook fish don't help dry hominy.
*An almost hooked fish does not improve
the taste of hominy grits.*

Man p'int, but God disap'pint.
*Man's plans are subject to the changes
that God places upon them.*

Tongue and teth don't always git along.

DE WATERMELON
(GULLAH LANGUAGE STORY)

In 1840, a runaway slave from Wallace Plantation was caught stealing watermelon on Fripp Plantation.

Some massa an some oberseer bery cruel. One nite, a man go in de feel to git wadar mellon. He be bery hongry for dey ain gib de slaves nuff to eat annee time. De guard catch him. Shut him up all dat day, wait fo high tide. Tide jes as high as tis now.
Den, he tak fo mens an dey duck him, an duck duck him an duck him twell he mos dead. Den dey lay him big log, an dey two mens hol arms up an tother mens hol he legs an de oberseer breat him till bled jes gush. An de womans an de mans an de chitlin all holler. "Yo gwine kell him." I knowed I ben stanin rite yere jes as it ben ye'tiddy. Den dey pit him in cart an him drive to de main road an dey den come to de certon spot. Dey trow him out like a bag manure an he lie rite dere an day clean he be dead.

De oberseer been rested an pit in de jail an dey gwing hung him, but de massa pay him out an let him go. Neber let him be comin back here dough.

slave woman

CROPS HARVESTED BY GULLAHS

1520 Figs, olives, oranges, peaches, apricots, grapes
1600 Pine, pitch turpentine, silk
1680 Rice
1750 Indigo
1790 Cotton
1830 Phosphate
1920 Free Gullahs: tomatoes, lettuce, cabbage, radish

Unsuccessful Crops: Ginger

GULLAH
TECHNOLOGY

Ham is a European Biblical word for Khem (Black), just as Nubia, Sudan, Moors, and Ethiopian are their words for Black Africans. The Khemetic Africans, dating back to 1.7 million BCE [Before Common Era] came from Southern Africa from an area commonly called Sudan. They traveled to Egypt (KMT) before 5,000 BCE A drought around the Sahara Desert area in 2,500 BCE caused some Africans to move to Europe, India, China, Japan, and the Middle East. Ancient Africans brought the concept of one God and knowledge (Karate, Acupuncture) and basically civilized the colored and white races. Despite this, the Europeans (whites) remain a predatory race that prey upon others' human and natural resources. Predators attack the weak as well as strong because they are hungry for food and/or resources. They taught Africa's greatest gift to the world, "Human Relationship." The East Khemetic languages are spoken by the ethnic groups of Somalia, Masai and Galla. The Galla (Gullah) moved to Africa's west coast. Galla were free Africans put into slavery by the Arabs and then the Europeans. They were not allowed to speak or write in African language, dress in African clothes, use African jewelry, artifacts, customs, ceremonies, rituals or treat women divinely. They could not use African moral values or their Khemetic religion (called Pagan Religion by Euro-Christians, Euro-Moslems, Euro-Jews) or practice "Maat" (truth, righteousness, and justice). Galla (Gullah) people brought their knowledge of "Human Relationship"and technology to America.

Dating back to 10,000 BCE and pre-Egypt, the documented ancient African skills and knowledge brought to America and the European world were many. They include engineering, agriculture, irrigation, the invention of the wheel, the zodiac, the fire sticks (matches), the process of boiling water, astronomy, navigation, mills, cultivation, the theater, construction, wheel barrow, metal (tin) work, carpentry, philosophy, music, cereals, the sail ships, pulleys, levers, massage, metric system, government, law, pants, medicine, physics, calculus, sewing, architecture, business, textile industry, bowling, tic-tac-toe, money, chemistry, herbology, plumbing, dance therapy, gymnastics, language pendulums, bureaucracy, kingmanship, chess, priesthood, religions, cosmetology, swings, toilet soap, fans, magnets, preservation of nature (ecology), fairy tales (rites of passage), writing, natural birth, pharmacology, farming tools, dentistry, ophthalmology, hot (green) house, steam bath, clock, civilization, etc.

Gullah people were given names based upon African ethnic groups that they came from, such as the Krio (called Creole) and the Kissi people (called Geechee).

GULLAH
HAG STORIES

Gullah "Hag" stories reflect African folk beliefs, and are firmly rooted in mythology and relate to wisdom, justice and spirituality. A "Hag" is a spirit that visits the living in order to transport information or messages from the spirit world. "Hags"are similar to an aura (electromagnetic cloud) and can be felt or in some way sensed to be present around the living. There are also "Bo-Hags." The African word "Bo" means far away, so a "Bo-hag" is a spirit (ancestral) from far away, Africa, or a deceased relative. Hag stories may seem like mumble jumble or super-stitions from slavery days. However, these stories carry keys to wisdom and are not as fragmented or irrelevant as they sound.

In ancient Africa, as well as Egypt, the aura was respected and acknowledged to be a living part of life. Gullah "Hag" stories reflect African culture and acknowledge that the aura (could be of deceased ancestors) is a living part of life. In fact, the aura, (called KA by Egyptians) is made primarily by the Pineal gland. The pineal gland makes a liquid called Melanin. The pineal gland is a pea-size gland in the center of the brain. Melanin makes an electromagnetic cloud, called an aura. This aura and melanin continuously vibrate during life and after a person's death. Melanin carries genetic information, influences all bodily activities, emotions, actions, thinking, growth, extrasensory perception, nerve impulses, muscles, metabolism and immunity, aside from giving African peoples' skin its black color. In any case, the "Hag" stories and legends have a vague connection to ancient African scientific information. The stories demonstrate how African science fragmentedly survived through an enslavement, which lawed and castrated African culture, science, and religion. The Hag stories are a testimonial to the Gullah's stubbornness to remain African and live as a spiritual people. Gullahs are spiritual people and they are able to feel or sense the presence of an aura. They have many stories for activities, misbehaviors, adventures and conversations with spirits or auras, commonly called "Hags."

In Egyptian Mythology, the first written Hag-type stories appear. For example, one such Hag story is about the Goddess Nut (pronounced Noot). Goddess Nut wanted to find out the secret power of Ra (Sun God). In the story, Ra represents the sun or the attribute of God to make living energy. Nut was the attribute of God to create. Goddess Nut created the sky or heaven. Ra became very old and always took long walks in order to look at his creations of the water, wind, plants, animals, and the earth. On one of his walks, Goddess Nut poisoned Ra with a dart, causing him to go into a deadly deep sleep. She told Ra she could save him from death if he gave her his secret powers. Ra eventually whispered the secret word of power into Nut's ear and she saved him from death. Nut, who was symbolically a Hag that used sleep or the time when the soul leaves the body to travel in order to get power. In this story, Ra and Nut represent the two great truths that each person must know. These truths were taught during "Rites of Passage" and are commonly known as Good/Evil, Right/Wrong, Man/Woman, Birth/Death, Night/Day,

Body/Spirt, etc. If a person is not following his spiritual purpose in a Godly life, then the Hag can disturb him, upset him, or take him in a deadly sleep. It was believed that the Hag (also called Hap, Hapi, etc.) was coming to transport the soul back to Africa, but the soul could not go unless it got rid of the Baraka (White Man's behavior or the ordeal).

The Hag story is also reflected in the name for the George Gershwin Gullah musical titled, *Porgy and Bess*. In Egyptian mythology, when Ra became an old man, he was given the name Bess. Traditionally, African Kings or Priests were responsible for communicating between the people and God. In other words, all the King's decisions were supposed to be checked by the will of God first and the legal system second. African Kings were given nicknames that symbolized communicating be-tween God and Earth. A fish symbolized transporting people's wishes, actions, and ideas between man and God. King Menes, of the First Egyptian Dynasty, was given the nickname Catfish (Porgy). Incidentally, Mene's name translates to Memphis. Therefore, the city of Memphis, Tennessee is named after this African man. In any case, the fish, Porgy, is a symbol directly related to Africa. Consequently, the title, *Porgy and Bess*, is directly related to Africa and the Hag's will to transport or take your spirit out of your body.

The origin of the word, Hag, can be found in the so-called *Egyptian Book of the Dead*, written 1500 BCE The correct name for the book is *The Book of Coming Forth by Day and by Night*. Hag is actually a distorted African word. Hag or Haxe or Hex stems from Hermes. Hermes means Thoth in the Egyptian language. Thoth is the spirit that reads the 42 negative confessions. The Ten Commandments are derived from the African 42 negative confessions. These confessions had to be answered correctly before a person's soul could enter heaven. Consequently, Hags like to read commandments, proverbs, newspapers, or scriptures. Hags are still secretly looking for the magic word of power in proverbs, newspapers, etc. Hags often sit down at a Hag stool (mushroom) to read. Gullahs would let mushrooms grow near their house so Hags could sit down and read instead of coming into the house.

Hags are believed to stop a restful sleep. The Hag may hold your body in a frozen position while you try to move your body. Hags may stop you from hollering out loud for help while in the midst of a horrible or dangerous nightmare. A Hag may disguise itself as a human being. Sometimes, it is believed that a Hag may possess a human body. Hags may take off the spirit skin and leave it outside your house before entering. There are tests to determine whether a person is a Hag. For example, sprinkle salt on the suspected Hag's shadow. If the person is a Hag, they will get nervous or shake or appear in pain. Sprinkle salt around the house and if a Hag takes off its skin, the salt will get in it and irritate them. Sometimes, a "Bad News Fly" or "Shoo Fly" will buzz around your head to warn you that a Hag is coming to your house or is in the house with you. In African Mythology, Shoo or Shun is the spirit that helps you to climb up the ladder (Jacob's ladder) in order to enter heaven. The "Shoo Fly" is trying to lift your spirit up or help you to be aware that a Hag is present. Some Hags like to drink alcohol and to enjoy parties. Hags may come to social gatherings and act like a clown or start trouble or a fight. You can lay a broom on the floor in the front doorway. This will stop a suspected hag from coming into your house. The broom can also stop a Hag from leaving your house. If someone stays in your house, eating up your food or talking a long time, or seems to be wearing out their welcome, they may be a Hag. It is best to put your broom behind the door and then the suspected hag will leave. Sometimes a Hag will hide in your clean clothes that are left outside on the clothesline overnight. Some Hags are bald and will use hair left in a comb to cover their bald heads or use the hair to make a person do something that the hag cannot do in its ghost form. It is usually advised to burn all hair left in your comb.

A few dogs or birds such as a crow can see hags. It is believed that the crow's hollering sound is "Hag! Hag!" It is believed that when a person sneezes, their soul may leave their body. If the Hag does not take the sneezing person's soul you traditionally say, "God Bless You." A safe way to protect the soul while sneezing is to say "Hag! Hag! Shoo!" This will stop a Hag from entering your body. It is good to carry a proverb or a favorite scripture in your pocket. Gullah slaves carried African words written on paper in Amulets and wore the Amulets around the neck. If a proverb, piece of newspaper or scripture was not available, then they would wear a little bag with a plant called, Asafoetida, in it. Asafoetida has a horrible smell and was called the Devil's Bowel Movement (dung). It has a smell that is similar to a rotten egg mixed with garlic and pig manure. Hags do not like the smell of Asafoetida and it is doubtful that you will like it either.

Hag stories hold traces of Gullah African heritage and fragments of the wisdom needed to live a family-centered life and a God-centered life. The use of the broom in Hag remedies symbolizes God because brooms were used to sweep African religious temples and to sweep the village compound before ceremonies and to bond marriages with God. The use of newspapers under beds, inside walls, or in shoes and the sprinkling of salt are related to a rich heritage. Hags are a fragment of a larger story of African origin. The Hag remedies can prevent a Hag from "tief" (stealing) you before "Day Clean"(morning) or drive you "crack-crack" (crazy) and broaden your appreciation of African culture.

DOMESTICATE
THE NEGRO
(THE PENN SCHOOL EXPERIMENT)

St. Helena Island's Penn School, like many schools on plantations, was started for the education of children and usually had African American teachers. The Gullah community started it on Oaks Plantation. Penn was supposed to be relocated on Port Royal Island, but was moved to Brick Church. Brick's one room eventually became too small for the student population. Churches from up north began sending supplies and missionaries. Eventually, it was relocated on the current Penn Center Campus. The Gullah teachers, like teachers of today, were dedicated to providing the best possible education within the European culture's standards. The educational focus of Penn started changing during the Civil War and focused upon teaching servitude labor. The Gullah community had the primary ingredients for independent Black businesses and needed to be pushed more in that direction; instead a dependent labor force was created.

The Gullah community was not consulted about how Penn School could serve their educational, social, financial or political needs. Historically, the school did not offer courses on how to establish cooperatives, factories, industry, colleges, banks, credit unions or political caucuses. This may have served the Gullah communities needs more humanely. Instead, the full force of government, missionaries, businessmen, and soldiers created a social caste and low-income class of domesticated Negroes in the name of an education experiment. The boys' "industrial" training meant laborers in crafts and trades that they said would enable the boys (men) to have a dignified living. The girls' (women) domestic science training meant work cleaning people's houses. Sometimes, the girls were sent to white male schools and dormitories to work and be sexually abused. These jobs for boys and girls were called "working out." This is a term for domestic work, working in fields, hotels, restaurants, packinghouses, oyster and shrimp factories. The domestication of Negroes or school training to "work out" was needed to keep Negroes living on the islands. This was believed to be a way to ensure that the Gullahs would not move to urban areas for jobs. A former instructor at Hampton Institute, Rossa Cooley, was brought to Penn to help make the experiment progress.

The Penn School domestication of Negroes was mislabeled a "test" of the Negro's ability to learn skills. Gullahs used these same skills for 450 years while they were slaves. It is well known that slaves operated, managed, supervised, negotiated business deals, were bookkeepers, craftsmen, agriculturists, and were sold as slaves because of technological skills. These skills, used by free Gullahs, led them to independence and had to be converted to servitude domestic laborers such as shoe repair, brick makers, cobbling, carpentry, harness-making, masons, potters, seamstresses, basket-sewers, wheelwrights, blacksmiths, and other skills needed by the white community. Donations, fund-raisers, Philanthropists, and religious groups, including fraudulent and deceptive money activities financed this domestication of the Negro.

Penn School had white groups, businesses, political organizations, and individuals continuously soliciting money to maintain and expand the school and services to the Black community. Penn accumulated large amounts of money from fundraising and donation schemes, which made whites rich while exploiting the students and community. Much of Penn's historical White criminal economic activities are shaded as benevolent or are falsely documented or not documented. However, the Penn Center Library still houses an abundance of proof of the economic activities. For example, in 1932, the wealth of Penn was $300,000. This money was supposed to go to the education of the enrolled 36 students and help the community. In the early 1940's Penn had 1 million dollars in money and assets, including land in Africa, railroad, textile mills, and a utility company in one account and $60,000 income in another account from rental properties owned in New Jersey, New York, and elsewhere. These monies amounted to more than enough to educate the students, establish Black-owned factories, industries, banks, colleges, etc. However, it is economically clear that the Negroes received none of the benefits. The whites used Penn School Negroes as a logo (identifying trademark) similar to the Negroes, Aunt Jemima on the pancake box and Uncle Ben on the rice box. Neither of these Negroes received a penny for their pictures, stimulating millions of dollars in sales. Penn Negroes were similarly used as logo bait to seduce whites and Blacks to donate monies.

The Penn School Negro logos (students) were used in a Wilhelmina Lynch (female version of Willie Lynch) strategy. With one exception from the Willie Lynch tactic, it pitted whites against whites. Willie Lynch is the name given to strategies for "seasonin" Africans. "Seasonin" is the cultural castration of Africans in order to give them the state of mind called a "slave" and the chained (chattel) or unchained behavior servitude (must have a White job, education, religion, culture, etc.) to White Supremacy. White Supremacy allows whites, as a gourp, to pass down from generation to generation the wealth created by slavery and captivity. A Black in captivity (i.e., Sea Island, Diaspora, in Africa) must follow the laws and customs of white civilization. A captive Black (chained or unchained) is a "slave" and every white becomes directly or indirectly a Slave Master (controls rewards and punishment of civilization). The method used to educate (indoctrinate) the Negroes and deceptively get donations are in the book, *The Art of War* by Thomas Cleary. Penn's continuous series of fundraising frauds and swindles used a cyclical logic diversion, which kept attention away from the perpetrators. The logic cycle started with:

1. Penn School being viewed by the public as a Church operation
2. Then, the Church was viewed as community-based, and then
3. The community was viewed as Penn School thus returning back to Step 1 in the cycle.

The cyclic logic diverts attention away from the whites and makes it impossible to directly blame them for crimes. It would be the same as blaming the Church and the Negroes. It must be kept in mind that the students, teachers and Gullah residents were not a part of or aware of the scam (fraudulent deceptive operations). In the "Wilhelmina Lynch" scam fund-raisers, political groups, donation accounts and businesses competed against and with each other to raise money to steal from the Negroes. The White owners of Penn School would get their share of the profits from scams and then give what amounts to peanuts to the Negroes.

In the past, Penn established a White-owned cooperative that serviced the Black community. The community could borrow money, pay interest on their loans and only get their loans if they used land as the collateral. The cooperative sold seeds that were donated to the community. The donated seeds, damaged fertilizers, money and other items were supposed to be given to the Gullahs. The damaged fertilizer destroyed corps, which caused further economic hardship on the Negroes and enabled the land to eventually be lost (collateral), to whites. Land was also lost due to nonpayment of taxes. For example, Charles E. Jenkins of St. Helena's Island would attempt to pay his $200 land tax, but was told at the tax office that he only had to pay $50. When Charles A. Jenkins would come to pay his $50 taxes, he would be told it was already paid. This eventually would cause both Jenkins to lose their land. Penn's solution to this scam was another scam. Penn raised money to pay the land taxes of the Jenkins' and other Blacks. Of course, Penn would loan the donated money to Blacks at interest and the loan was secured by using the land as collateral. If the Blacks did not have money to pay off the loan, then they would become an indenture slave laborer and work to pay off the debt. In some cases, if their labor failed to cover the loan Penn (i.e., affiliated business or company) would get the land and profit from the free labor. In another scam, Penn convinced the State to build a series of small schools. The Penn affiliated construction company was contracted to build them. The supplies were donated. Penn told the State that each school would cost $200 in construction supplies (was donated = free supplies) and labor (which was basically free). However, upon completion of the schools, Penn overcharged and inflated the price to $800 per school in order to extort more money in the scam. The success of this "Wilhelmina Lynch" money laundry tactic and domestication of the Negroes was well known. Officials from other states, countries, and school systems visited Penn to copy the domestication techniques and scams.

Penn Normal Industrial Agriculture School shifted from a normal academic European education to crafts and trades between 1900 and 1904. In 1950, Penn School officially ended its educational function. Penn produced good graduates and had teachers with pride in Gullah culture and a deep love for God. Today, Gullah culture and Penn is being used to bring tourist dollars to the area. The African Americans that visit the area get a sense of cultural pride. However, the major tourist dollar does not directly benefit the Gullah residents. Gullah culture is becoming a European American business.

What the Gullahs do get amounts to peanuts. No retribution to the Gullah communities has ever been made for past scams and violent crimes perpetrated by Penn's whites and other whites. The sum total of the scam crimes and cultural castration amounts to a driveby shooting of the Gullahs. It is only because of the grace of God, the many Harriet Tubman- and Nat Turner-type individuals that Gullah culture has survived.

EGYPTIAN ORNAMENTATION FOR A CEILING.

Gullah
Basket Making

Sea grass basket making is an ancient African art form that Gullah slaves brought to America. Basket making was part of the necessary crafts on plantations from Florida's St. John River to North Carolina's Cape Fear. However, more than 90 percent of the basket makers for rice plantations were concentrated in South Carolina and Georgia. A slave with the ability to make coiled grass, plaited palmetto and split oak baskets sold at higher prices than field laborers. Making grass implements and baskets was a functional part of life that survived slavery because of its artistic value and usefulness. The various African styles and techniques of sea grass baskets symbolize spirituality, consciousness and the academics of growth and development (so-called Rites of Passage). Baskets reveal a rich culture, lifestyle and heritage.

Ancient African baskets date back to 5000 BCE The African written language Medu Netcher (so-called Hieroglyphics) uses a sea grass basket for the symbol for the letter "K" as well as the letter "nb" and the words "every," "any," and "all." This indicates that basket weaving is at least as old as African languages (5 million years old). In Africa, baskets were used for sieves, storage of food, herbs, utensils and clothing. The ancient African Atlantic and Pacific shipping industry, camel and elephant caravans used baskets. The ancient Herb Shops (erroneously called Flower Shops) used sea grass frames for medicinal bouquets, reefs, neck collars and candle decorations.

The scent from herb stems, roots and flowers was called aromatic therapy. Aromatic therapy also used fragrance oils applied to baskets, rugs and mats. Herbs, such as eucalyptus, sandalwood, chamomile, water lily, clover, licorice, fennel, cinnamon, pepper-mint, rosemary, carob and lavender were used.

Doctor Athotis, the son of Menes, the Pharaoh of Egypt (3200 B.C.E.) used herbs and woven baskets, frames and utensils. Doctor Imhotep of the Third Dynasty (2980 B.C.E.), Doctor Hesy Ra (2600 B.C.E.) and Doctor Preshet (2600 B.C.E.) used sea grass woven items. Incidently, Doctor Preshet was one of the first women doctors in recorded history. Ancient African baskets have been found in the Theban Tomb of the 18th Dynasty, King Tutankhamen (King Tut) 14 B.C.E., King Thuthmosis III, and King Akenaten (Amenophis IV). In the "Feast of the Valley" festival, honoring Queen Hatshepsut, grass woven mats and baskets were used. Ramesse III of Egypt offered bread in a grass basket to honor Amun-Ra. His name was said after prayers and was distorted to the word Amen. The usage of baskets, collars and mats are in the Egyptian Book of the Dead. Paintings in the pyramid and coffin text show the mythological God Osirius and Goddess Isis sitting on thrones in chairs that may be resting on sea grass mats. In ancient Africa, some baskets were made of Cyperus, Papyrus, and Dom Palm. In contemporary times, Gullah basket making dates back as far as 1672. Fanners are listed in the Charleston County register of Wills and Inventories of Noah Serre on May 18, 1730.

Basket making was a family-centered art. Each family had unique styles of designing baskets. Unique designs can be traced to a specific tribe (i.e.,

Ashanti, Senegambia, Mende, Angolans, Yoruba, Twa, Gola, etc.). Each individual added their personal artistic signature to their work. The learning of basket making was experiental (learning by doing). It focused on the basic steps of making a knot, starting a coil, feeding grass, adding new strips of palmetto and finally making the basket "end off." Women usually made household type baskets for serving, storing utensils and food, and decorative functional artifacts. Men usually made large heavy baskets for thatching; reedwork; sieves; fish traps; drying trays; granary utensils; rugs; harvesting of corn, yams, potatoes, rice and cotton; and bushel baskets. However, during slavery, the demand for the heavier baskets needed for field work caused basket making to become mostly a man's art.

The basic grass for basket making is called Rush (Juncus Roemerianus) or needle grass, bulrush or rushel. It is stronger and more durable than sweet grass or pine straw and grows in sea water marsh. It is harvested by cutting with a rice hook and then dried. It is usually coiled in a bundle and bound together by stitching a binder around the bundle. Usually, the coil starts at the center of the bottom of a basket and the bundles are wrapped over each other like a coiling snake. This spiral coiling snake design symbolizes man's consciousness. It also represents the continuous presence of God in all aspects of life. The wrapping of bound coiled bundles with palmetto leaves is similar to a vine plant wrapping itself around a tree. The other basket making technique of plaiting or the intertwining of grass in a hair braid method symbolizes the ancient African Caduceus. The ancient African Caduceus (intertwined snakes) is used as the medical symbol. Single and double-row basket handles resemble the intertwined snakes. The overall repetitive horizontal and vertical designs and units represent birth and rebirth.

The stitching of grass baskets requires that split palmetto or oak is tied onto the previous stitch. The stitch is then pulled through almost to the end of its length. Then, the end of the previous binder and added binder are tucked between the row. Next, the new bundle is tightly wrapped with splits before a new stitch is started.

A "nail bone" or "bone" is the tool used to pull the binder through the coil foundation and for making the palmetto strips. Nail bones can be made by bagging needles, rib bones of hogs or cows, broken scissors or the neck of a teaspoon.

The fanner baskets are the most popular. They were usually carried on the head with foodstuff or other items inside. The fanners were used for separating chaff separated from the rice in a mortar with a pestle. This pounded and threshed brown rice was poured into the fanner then tossed up into the air 12 inches or more and then caught in the Fanner or poured into a basket on the ground. This allowed the chaff to be blown away from the brown rice. Fanners can be up to 20 inches in width, 3 inches in height and in a saucer shape. They are coiled rush, sewn with oak splits or strips of cabbage palm leaves or palmetto butt or leaves. Sometimes, they are made of coiled rice straw and corn shuck. Today, fanners are made for decoration. Gullahs no longer eat the brown rice. Instead, they eat synthetic processed white rice which is robbed of 90 percent of its nutrients and fiber. Once the brown rice is processed, it becomes a type of synthetic white dirt (junk food similar to bleached white flour, white grits, and white sugar). This is a constipating and diabetes causing food.

Baskets sometimes have lids. In ancient African culture, the baskets with a "steeple-top" (lid) represent the pyramid or consciousness of God. Typically, most churches have pyramid-shaped steeple roofs. Pyramids produce static electricity aside from symbolizing spirituality. Many baskets have lids such as lunch, trash, bread, sewing, cake, vegetable steamer and hamper baskets. Aside from these grass-woven baskets, there are handbags, shopping bags, hat boxes, potpourri and flower baskets.

The African origin of sea grass baskets is noted in the Charleston Chamber of Commerce pamphlet, published in 1938. Alfred Graham, a basket making teacher at Penn School, said that he learned the art from his African father. Basket making is rooted in African civilization. It stands as a Gullah monument that ancient Africans were not primitive, pagan savages from a dark continent.

Finding of wells, sweet grass basket weaving, and carrying items on the head are parts of African Gullah culture
(Margaret McDonald Sanders)

Gullah
Herb Medicine

Gullah herbal medicine is based upon the ancient African Art (Female Principle) and Science (Male Principle) of holistic medicine. Herb treatments require knowledge of the spiritual, mental, and physical (holistic) aspects of dis-ease and wellness. Africa is the origin of holistic herb medicine. The oldest books on health are the African books racistly mislabeled and given European names such as the *Kahum Medical Papyrus* (1700 BCE), *Edwin C. Smith Papyrus* (1600 BCE) and *Ebers Medical Papyrus* (1550 BCE). Gullah medicine, due to slavery/colonialism is diluted because African peoples' languages, holistic medicine, religions, and Maat culture was and is constantly made diluted and dysfunctional by White Supremacy. This brief listing of herb remedies can be prepared singularly or in combinations by using the measurement of 1 teaspoon to a cup of water. Herb roots, barks, berries, and seeds are boiled at low heat (simmered) for an hour or more while herb leaves and flowers are put in boiling hot water and allowed to soak (steep) for an hour then strained and drank. These herbs are effective and can be purchased in pill or liquid extract form and used singularly or in combination. The asterisk (*) indicates popular herbs used for a remedy.

Arthritis/Rheumatism
Angelica
Cherry Bark
Button Snakeroot
Poke Root (Berries)
Sassafras*
Burdock*

Burns/Ulcers (Sores)
Garlic
Cow Dung (Applied)
Comfrey*
Elderberry
Life Everlasting
Sutras

Bites
Elderberry (Apply for Chigger)
Ironweed (Snake)
Angelica Tree (Snake)

Colds/Asthma
Black Root
Boneset
Button Snakeroot
Horehound*
Life Everlasting*
Mullein*
Nightshade
Brown Muckle (Bayberry)
Poke Root
Pine Tar
Speedwell

Sweet Gum (Fruit)
St. John
White Snakeroot
Groundselbush/White Muckle/Sea Myrtle

Circulation (Poor)
Bloodroot

Cramps
Mint (Stomach)
Life Everlasting
Sampson's Snakeroot
Ayshaberry/Black Cohosh (Female)

Cuts
Elderberry
Senna (Apply)
Sutras
Spider Web (Apply)

Constipation
Senna*
Okra

Diuretic
Aloe
Kidney Weed
Jerusalem Artichoke
Button Snakeroot

Diarrhea
Blackberry
Horsenettle
Sampson's Snakeroot

Diabetes
Peach Leaves
Blue Raspberry leaves/Huckleberry/Bilberry*

Female Problems
(Fibroids, Endometriosis, etc.)
Ayshaberry/Black Cohosh (Estrogen)*
Dandelion Root*
Burdock Root*
Red Clover*
Saw Palmetto Berry*
St. John
Nightshade

Fever
Bitter Apple
Boneset
Ironweed
Life Everlasting*
Muckle
Mullein*
Tadawas
Whiteroot
Fever (Oil) Bush (Bath)

Griping
Blackberry
Dog Fennel*
Ginger*

Headaches
Indian Shot (Lady's Slipper)
White Willow*

Heart Trouble
Black Cohosh
Hyssop
Chamomile

Hair Rinse
Mistletoe
Pine Needles*
Nettle (Also drank for hair growth)*

High Blood Pressure
Hyssop*
Black Cohosh
Garlic*
Boneset
Saw Palmetto Berries
Spanish Moss (Put in shoes)

Itch
Hairy Laurel

Measles
Chickweed
(Also used for controlling the appetite and colds)

Menstruation
(Decrease flow)
Brown Muckle (Bayberry)
Cherry Bark
Horsenettle
Comfrey
Red Oak (Pain, douche for prolapsed uterus)
Cotton Root (Small amount eases labor, large
amount causes abortion)

Muscle Pain / Sprains
White Willow*
Fennel (Apply to area)
Swamp Grass
Mullein
Boneset

Pain
Life Everlasting (Foot pain)
Mint (Stomach pain)
White Willow (All areas)

Poultices
Clay and Moss
Onion and Clay

Sting
Fennel
Tobacco (Apply)
Galax

Swelling
Brown Muckle (Bayberry)
Jimson Weed
Mullein
Chinaberry

Ticks
Red Muckle

Tonic
Sassafras
Mullein
Life Everlasting
Ayshaberry
Dandelion Root

Worms
Ayshaberry/Black Cohosh
Button Snakeroot
Jimson
Sampson's Snakeroot
Garlic

Warts
(Skin Disease, Fibroids, Endometriosis, Sarcadosis)
Cedar Wood / Thuja
(Drink and/or apply to area)

ROOTWORK:
DR. BUZZARD

The Sea Islands, African American communities, slave plantations and African civilization have Root Doctors. Rootwork currently exists in Black communities. Doctor Buzzard is a title given to a Root Worker. This aspect of African culture has been distorted and misunderstood because of "Seasonin" (Brainwash). Slaves lost the original Rites of Passage used to enter the guild, lost the Kemetic prescriptions, herbs and tools. There have been many to exploit and misrepresent the science. Let's look at a few examples of Rootwork prescriptions.

Luck
Get a red onion. Cut a small hole in the onion. Put five coins in the hole. Soak the onion, with the coins in it overnight in a tea made of High John the Conqueror (Bloodroot or Red Root). The next day, take the coins out of the onion. Take the coins with you when you gamble (i.e., Bingo, Lottery, etc.). The coins make your five fingers lucky.

Escape a Love Spell:
Get a picture of the person or a witness, such as a piece of their hair or something they have touched or worn. Mix the witness with grave-yard dirt and ashes from burnt Asefoctida. Throw the mixture at a crossroads or a road leading out of town.

Turning de Trick:
Write the person's name on paper backwards, three times. Put the paper and Devil's Claw in a jar. Bury the jar in the cemetery at night. If the trick or spell involves your car, money, job, always losing things, sex, etc., then write that word backwards, three times and follow the steps.

The psycho-spiritual practitioners of this science have many titles, such as Root Doctor, Conjurer, Santerian (usually Cuban, Puerto Rican), Murdumugas Abinzas (Sudan), Hoodoo, Voodoo (Haiti), Shaman, Condomble (Brazil), JuJu, Curanderos, Priest/Priestess, Shango (Trinidad), Ngangas, Mojo, Doctor Buzzard (Sea Islands), Pukumina and Obea (Jamaica), Sorcerer, Marabouts, Occultist, etc. Many are traditional health practitioners, while some are perpetrating a fraud. These practitioners use herbs, witnesses, rituals, cere-monies, incantations, psychic ability, trances, theater, music, hypnotism, eggs, nails, trees, water, metal, graveyard dirt, shells, bones, forks, shoes, hats, stones, coins, drums, candles, incense, bells, psychology, electromagnetic aura science, spells, etc. There are many ancient books (erroneously called *Papyrus*) that document this art such as *Leyden Papyrus, Ebers Papyrus, Salt Papyrus, Ani Papyrus (Egyptian Book of the Dead)*, etc.

The practitioner may use the electromagnetic melaninated energy of a person. This type of energy is also called acupuncture meridians, chakras, chi, prana, Akasic, aura, life force, etc. The energy is specific and similar to an individual's fingerprint. This electromagnetic impression is left upon anything an individual touches, feels, fears, and believes. It is on the individual's photograph, hair, clothing, audio tape of an individual's voice, handwriting, etc. It is sometimes called a *witness* to an individual's existence. Historically, there have been many Africans that have used the science.

In history, many African counterattacks (so-called slave rebellions and revolts) against the Race War (the whites' military invasion, colonization of Africa and enslavement of Blacks) involved practitioners. The combined European countries' continuous military invasion, murder, enslavement, capture, inferiorization and colonialization of all Black people are, by definition, a Race War. Warriors that fought in the Race War, such as Toussaint L'Ouverture, were considered Root Doctors. He used conjuring to give his Haitian army added strength to counterattack and kill the Whites to gain freedom.

In 1751, conjurer and psychic Chief/Priest MacKandal of Haiti, was a military scientist and root worker practitioner that used his skills to organize a counterattack on the slave plantation. In 1791, conjurers and military scientists Priest Boukman and Lamour Derance, used spells in their counterattack (Revolt). In 1822, the Minister of Defense for Denmark Vesey, was a practitioner named Gullah Jack. He used his root work and military skills in the counterattack in Charleston, South Carolina. In 1831, Nat Turner's counter-attack, in Virginia, involved practitioners. David Walker was known to be a Pan-Africanist and a practitioner of the Art/Science of Psycho-spirituality. George Washington Carver, a modern day Alchemist, used conjuring. He was known to say that the plants told him what to do. The many known and nameless practitioners were able to influence and alter events and lives of enslaved and freed Africans because they used a technology that is a fundamental part of African culture.

The root worker practitioner must diagnose the disease, find the cause, and prescribe a remedy. They must distinguish whether the disease is from natural causes, i.e., diet, drugs, an organ malfunction, constipation, toxins, etc.; Supernatural, i.e., ancestors, arisha, spirit illness, the double = KA, etc.; and Preternatural, i.e., spell, jinx, curse, hex, etc.

After the practitioner diagnoses the illness, they must

- Tell who do it to you (Who Do = Hoodoo)
- Find the witness (item used, such as egg, bottle, wood, food, etc.
- Tell whether it is a Hex, Spell, Evil Eye, Curse, Cross, etc. or whether another practitioner did it;
- Reverse the Hex = Double the Cross, Turn the Bible, Turn the Trick;
- Give a treatment and remedy = cure.

It is a very sensitive science and directly puts the practitioner in just as much danger as the client (victim).

Many Africans are too ashamed of conjurers and deny that spells exist, but are too afraid to challenge it. There are those that did not believe that the African science of hypnotism actually worked. If they were hypnotized in front of an audience and after being taken out of a hypnotic trance, they would deny that hypnotism worked. Many Africans have been and/or are currently under a conjurer's spell. They mistranslate and misexplain conjurers' spells as bad luck, fate and punishment for past deeds. Many adult and children's physical and mental illnesses are caused by spiritual imbalances or conjurers. These illnesses are ignorantly treated with surgery, drugs, and psychology.

The majority of the Doctor Buzzard practitioners are sincere and use some form of Maat (reciprocity, justice, righteousness, solidarity, hope, fairness) in helping people. Historically, Africans never have had fear of spirits, magic, spells, curses, hoodoo, mojo or the metaphysical (supernatural). Africans have accepted that harm could be done by unseen forces and/or negative thinking. Most of the African natural practitioners, midwives, naturopaths, herbalists and natural nutritionists know of the conjurer science. Some use it and many do not. The African focus has shifted to divination, psychics, fortune-telling, evil tricks, love potions, sacrifices, luck, winning money, etc. The stores exploit this Africanism by charging high prices for conjurer artifacts that can change life's circumstances such as cheap egg-dyed water, candles, alcohol and water mixtures, white sugar mixtures, synthetic chemicals, decorative and medicinal herbs and harmless homemade-type concoctions. The true value and power of this African science is being polluted, commercialized, destroyed and put in a cultural crisis.

The isolation of Gullahs on the Sea Islands has allowed them to keep aspects of the conjurer science alive. Many traces of Root Work concepts, as well as practices are alive among all Africans. Many Africans deny that it exists because they have become Afropeans (Seasonin = Civilized = Domesticated). It is similar to the fragmented trace of the Council of the Elders (Wise).

During slavery the prisoners of the Race War (slaves) would meet at a large tree or in a slave cabin to discuss and debate community issues, bank money, solve conflicts, counsel others and argue issues. In the cities, the meetings would be held under a special tree and in absence of a tree, the meetings would be held on the corner. The children would gather on the corner and imitate the Elders. Boys would have mock meetings on the corner, imitating the Elders are called Corner Boys. The original cause of the mock meetings is lost and the conversation has taken on forms of self-hatred, cursing Mother Africa (referred to as "Your Momma") and reinforcement of Slavery Trauma. The "Dozens" is played on the corner. The "Dozens" is a slave game of belittling and degrading each other in a competitive fashion. The participants try to make the onlookers laugh. Originally, the mentally and physically diseased or handicapped Africans were sold by the Dozen at slave auctions. The Auctioneer would describe the slave's defect. For example, this slave is so retarded that he cannot chew and walk at the same time. The children, in their mock behavior, are pointing back to slavery and African history, lifestyle, and culture. The traces of the Council of Elders cannot be denied just as Gullah culture and conjurers can still be found interwoven into the fabric of African American lifestyles.

Slave Children *photograph circa Emancipation*

BIBLIOGRAPHY

Adams, J.T. *Dictionary of American History.* New York: Schribner and Sons, 1940.

Amponsah, K. *Topics on West African Traditional Religion.* Accra, Ghana: McGraw-Hill, 1974.

Aptheker, H. *Afro-American History: The Modern Era.* Citadel Press, Inc., 1971.

Avalon Hill Game Company. Baltimore, Maryland.

Baskin, W. *Dictionary of Black Culture.* Philosophical Library, Inc., 1973.

Beaufort Arsenal Museum. Beaufort, South Carolina.

Bierrer, B.W. *South Carolina Indian Lore.* Columbia, South Carolina: Bert N. Bierrer, 1972.

Boorstin, D. *The Discoverers.* New York: Random House, 1983.

Carruth, G. *The Encyclopedia of American Facts and Dates.* T. Crowell Company, 1972.

Conrad, Earl. "General Tubman, Composer of Spirituals," *Etude Magazine,* LX (May, 1942), 305 f.

Crum, M. *Gullah Negro Life in the Carolina Sea Islands.* Durham, North Carolina: Duke University Press, 1940.

Dabbs, E. *Sea Island Diary.* Spartanburg, South Carolina: The Reprint Company, 1983.

Fu-Kiau, K., A.M. Lukondo-Wamba. *Kindezi: The Kongo Art of Babysitting.* New York, NY: Vantage Press, 1988.

Genovese, Eugene. *From Rebellion to Revolution.* Vintage Books, 1981.

Hayden, Robert. *Eight Black American Inventors*. Addison Wesley Publishing Company, 1972.

Holt, Thomas. *Black Over White*. University of Illinois Press, 1979.

Jones, P.J. *South Carolina: One of the Fifty States*. Sandlapper Publishers, Inc., 1985.

Joyner, Charles. *Down by the Riverside*. University of Illinois Press, 1984.

Kane, J. *Famous First Fact*. New York: The H. W. Wilson Company, 1964.

Koger, L. *Black Slaveowners*. Jefferson, North Carolina: McFarland and Company, Inc., 1958.

Mannix, Daniel. *Black Cargoes: A History of the Atlantic Slave Trade*. Viking Press, 1962.

McGaffey, W. *Custom and Government in Lower Congo*. Berkeley, California: University of California Press, 1970.

Mitchell, Faith. *Hoodoo Medicine*. Reed, Cannon and Johnson Company, 1978.

Morrow, Willie. *400 Years Without a Comb*. San Diego, California: Black Publishers, 1973.

Morshead, O.F., *The Diary of Samuel Pepys*. New York: Harper and Brothers, 1926.

New York Times, August 6, 1865.

Nunez, B. *Dictionary of Afro-American Civilization*. Greenwood Press, 1980.

Parsons, R.T. *Religion in African Society*. Leiden E. J. Brill, 1904.

Petit, J.P. *South Carolina and the Sea maritime and Ports*. Charleston, South Carolina: Activities Committee, 1976.

Postell, W.D. *The Health of Slaves on Southern Plantations*.

Rose, Julio. *Heru-Tage Ra-Staured Heru-Scope*. Cayce, SC: Starlight Communication, 1997.

Rose, W. *Rehearsal for Reconstruction: The Port Royal Experiment*. Indianapolis, Indiana: Boobs-Merrill, 1964.

The South Carolina Historical Chronicle

Tindall, G.B. *South Carolina Negroes, 1877-1900*. University of South Carolina Press, 1952.

Waring, J.L. *A History of Medicine in South Carolina*.

Williams, Chancellor. *The Destruction of Black Civilization*. Chicago, Illinois: Third World Press, 1976.

Index